Kim is a very talented, very global executive who has been developing people around the world for the last 20 years. Her ability to simplify and her courage to communicate on any topic make her a great partner. This book opens the vault to Kim's insight.

— SYD FINKELSTEIN, Steven Roth Professor of Management, Tuck School of Business at Dartmouth College, and author of *Why Smart Executives Fail*

Kim Janson takes the complex subjects of talent management and development and makes them simple, insightful, and replicable in *Demystifying Talent Management*. This book is a valuable resource for those that want to excel in managing and developing people.

— BILL JOHNSON, former Chairman, President, and CEO, H.J. Heinz Company

Having worked closely with Kim at Hasbro, especially in building the Tuck Executive Leadership Program with her, she remains my top choice as a leadership development partner. Her book does a great job of taking the often confusing genre of managing or developing people and distilling the key ideas that, if you use them, will help make you a powerful leader.

— ALAN HASSENFELD, Chairman of the Executive Committee and former CEO, Hasbro

As a CEO, I've read many books on developing people and managing better. Kim Janson's *Demystifing Talent Management* rises to the top because of the comprehensiveness and connectedness of the message and the simplicity in which it is laid out. The book is powerful because it is a simple, straight-forward message for managers on what and how to do things for high impact.

— AL VERRECCHIA, former CEO and Chairman, Hasbro

Getting talent management right is an imperative to succeed in the marketplace today. Kim Janson is an accomplished professional with an impressive track record of helping companies deliver practical, high-impact talent management programs and processes. In *Demystifying Talent Management,* she shares her insights and experiences. I recommend this book as a great resource to anyone looking to improve their talent management efforts.

— KEVIN WILDE, Chief Learning Officer and Vice President, Organizational Effectiveness, General Mills, and Executive Leadership Fellow, Carlson School of Management, University of Minnesota

Demystifying Talent Management is a gem. Kim's straightforward, no-nonsense approach is refreshing. Very few can cut through the clutter and jargon like she can. Being an effective manager, particularly of top talent, is not easy. Kim provides simple, easy-to-use and intuitive tools and strategies to get the very best out of your people. If you want to build a high-performing team, this book is a must read.

— STEVE CLARK, former Senior Vice President and Chief People Officer, H.J. Heinz Company

Over the last nearly 20 years of working with organizations of all sizes and industries, I have never been more impressed with an approach to talent management as I have been with the the systems that Kimberly Janson has installed. Practical, insightful, simple and yet immensely effective; Kimberly's designs and her leadership have benefitted all levels of the organization. She is an impressive professional and I am so glad she has shared her work so others can experience her models.

— DAVE MITCHELL, Founder and President, The Leadership Difference

Working with Kim is game changing. She applies laser focus to determine the dynamics of a situation and quickly diagnoses how to address things. A book from Kim on managing and developing people is a powerful read because she applies these skills, adds her direct style, and in the end you have a very clear, compelling how-to manual.

— RON GARROW, Chief Human Resources Officer, Mastercard

Experienced-based, storytelling approach used to humanize the tools and techniques to effectively LEAD and DEVELOP top talent.

— DAVE WOODWARD, Founder, Woodward Leadership Ltd, and former Executive Vice President, President, and CEO - Europe, H.J. Heinz Company

This book is fantastic! Kim's thought leadership, expertise and extensive experience are reflected in the content of this book. She takes complex talent management concepts and makes them understandable and easy to execute. If you are a leader and follow Kim's advice, you'll build the talent required to fuel growth.

— JIM SHANLEY, President, The Shanley Group, and former Staffing, Learning, and Development Executive, Bank of America

Kim brings deep global experience, earned across many industries, to the critical but often under-leveraged skill of talent management. Her book draws on this practical experience, and is a clear, pragmatic blueprint for effectively coaching and developing people. Kim's simple, direct, and insightful messages are excellent lessons, and reminders, to anyone trying to get the most out of people and drive for sustainable, long-term success.

— ART WINKLEBLACK, former Executive Vice President & Chief Financial Officer, H.J. Heinz Company

There is oftentimes an air of mystic that swirls around conversations relating to talent and capability development in corporations. I have often wondered why this is. Picking the best talent for the Saturday football game or the next drama production seems at times to be so much easier than driving succession inside a large multinational corporation. Yet the results that both processes aim to address are the same, the best performance that is possible and, ultimately, success. Finding a way to have the real conversations relating to talent, authentic and at times challenging discussions, and in a way that breaks open the topic and targets clear, measurable, and above all sustainable progress lies at the heart of demystifying the subject. Kimberley Janson has cracked the code, a skill that she has honed, applied, and proven in a range of national and global corporations. To now have the opportunity to share in Kim's practical and proven insights is a pleasure for leaders and students alike. For those that have grappled with this subject and are looking for the impetus to hone their own performance in this essential of all leadership areas, or for those that seek to better understand how things really can and do drive results when the most effective of practices are understood and applied, Kim's work is a must read. I know – I have been coached by, have benefitted from, and have seen Kim's words translated into concrete actions and results!

— BRYCE DYER, Vice President Human Resources, GlaxoSmithKline

Kim is a straight shooter and her book is written the way she coaches – direct, practical, and humorous. As always, she creates accountability for your own success in using her advice.

— LOUISE KORVER, former Head of Leadership & Executive Development at Ingersoll Rand, Bank of America, EMC, and AT&T

As an HR professional for almost 30 years, I have had the opportunity to work as an HR business partner for outstanding leaders in very successful multinational companies. But every time I tried to get in place either a piece of activity or system linked to people, I received from them questions like: Why do I need it? Are we overcomplicating the work? How do these different systems work together? Finally, we have a book that can address all these questions in a very simple and clear language that even non-HR managers can understand. The scheme that Kimberly Janson has created to summarize the activities related to managing and developing people is impressive: clear, simple and effective. Read the book and get a complete picture of how to successfully develop people and business. You can get at a glance all the activities a company has to put in place if its senior leaders want to be successful and want to bring their employees to their peak! That is what the book is about: helping people unleash their potential to achieve peak performance. I recommend it to HR managers who are looking for a simple way to explain to their business partners how all the different HR activities work together. I recommend it to senior managers who want to understand the total picture of the people-related system. I recommend it to people who want to learn how they can be more successful or how they can better motivate their people.

— VALENTINO D'ANTONIO, HR Director - Italy and Global Infant & Nutrition, H.J. Heinz Company

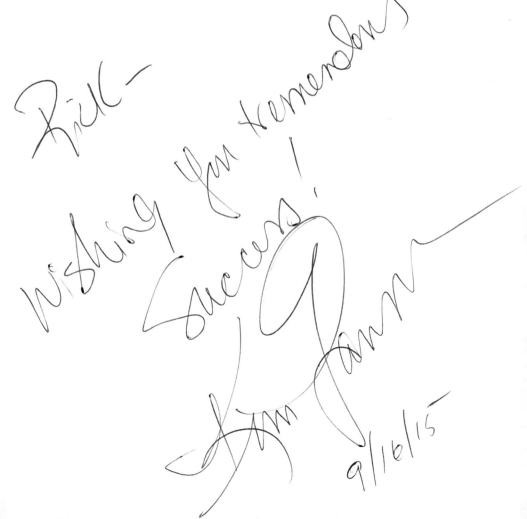

DEMYSTIFYING
Talent
Management

Unleash People's Potential to
Deliver Superior Results

Kimberly Janson

MAVEN HOUSE
PRESS

Published by Maven House Press, 4 Snead Ct., Palmyra, VA 22963; 610.883.7988; www.mavenhousepress.com.

Special discounts on bulk quantities of Maven House Press books are available to corporations, professional associations, and other organizations. For details contact the publisher.

While this publication is designed to provide accurate and authoritative information in regard to the subject matter covered, it is sold with the understanding that the publisher is not engaged in rendering legal, accounting, or other professional service. If legal advice or other expert assistance is required, the services of a competent professional person should be sought. — From the Declaration of Principles jointly adopted by a Committee of the American Bar Association and a Committee of Publishers and Associations

Library of Congress Control Number: 2014957205

Paperback ISBN: 978-1-938548-30-7
ePUB ISBN: 978-1-938548-31-4
ePDF ISBN: 978-1-938548-32-1

Printed in the United States of America.

10 9 8 7 6 5 4 3 2 1

CONTENTS

DEDICATION

THIS BOOK is dedicated to my parents. My dad, Raymond Hill, inspired me to think that nothing is beyond my reach. My mom, Elizabeth Hill, is always there with a laugh and a net whenever I stumble. I won the parent lottery for sure.

A Note of Thanks

In the spirit of believing we don't thank people enough for what they bring to our lives, please indulge me while I say thanks to my community.

I believe it takes a village to be successful, and I am so grateful for mine. I have many people to thank for my success. My husband, Mike, is my rock. Everyone will tell you what a great guy he is, and I'm fortunate that he has spent his life holding my hand or walking behind me with a broom to clean up the messes I leave. He's truly a gift. My children, Michael and Hannah, are the motivation behind everything I do. The best thing I will ever do with my life is to be their mom. They make me better, make me laugh, and make me proud.

Thanks to my amazing sisters – Patt, Beth, Linda, Kate, Cindy, and Reen – who are always there for me. Thanks to my brothers, Ray, Rick, and Steve – especially Rick and his wicked wife, Anita – who have been valuable supporters. Thanks to my husband's family and his mom, Jean, especially. Thanks to my nieces and nephews (there are over twenty of them!). You make me better by making me want to be a good role model for you. My nephew Chris once said to his mom, "Mom, if I have a problem I will definitely call you. But if I have a real problem, I'm calling Aunt Kim." Ha! Love that!

I'm blessed to have so many wonderful friends and colleagues. Michael Block, in his hilarity, can make me laugh at any darn moment. The only moment of laughter during the funeral of my beloved father was when Michael, who is Jewish, got in line for communion because he thought he was going to get some food. I can name so many people – Sharon Lively, Jacques Pradel, Steve Clark, Linda Miklas, David Oliynyk, Raquel Powers, Dave Cotrone, Dianna Azzolina, Jan Kruise, Joanne Haworth, Sandra Drought, June Youngs, David Bailin, Darcie Zeliesko, Jackie Boucher, Paul Valliere – and so many more, and I would still be short by at least 3,000 names – these are all of the wonderful people I have benefited from being near.

Thanks to all of the people who have provided input, through the years, that has added to this book, and to those who took the time to take part in the survey and interviews I conducted. Thanks to the fabulous people who looked at the manuscript when it was about 80 percent complete to be sure I was making my points clearly. Thanks to those who believed in me and gave me their endorsements. Thanks to my community of supporters on Facebook who were always a source of encouragement. Thanks to Mark Holman, my equine vet, who every time I saw him asked, "How's the book coming?" While the interest was sincere, the question was a little push and, because I admire Mark very much, I appreciated it every time. Thanks so much to my literary agent, Ken Lizotte, who procured six contracts from six different publishing houses to publish the book. This was such an inspiration that it made writing it easy. Thanks to the great publisher we decided to partner with, Jim Pennypacker of Maven House Press – you couldn't have made it easier.

— Kim Janson

PART I

Overview

CHAPTER ONE

What You're In For

WHY THIS BOOK? The idea of unleashing people's potential by giving them good input and stretching them to new levels is heady stuff. To help people dig deep and uncover what's inside them and then watch them become successful is highly rewarding. Done consistently and thoroughly with a group or an organization, it's incredibly powerful. The collective impact of employees performing at the highest level and truly working TOGETHER is limitless. The magic that can happen when the constraints that organizations put on their own people (or that we put on each other or on ourselves) are removed makes for extraordinary results.

Who wouldn't want to be part of unleashing people's potential? So why is it that lack of direction, lack of development, lack of good coaching and feedback, and poor work environments appear as major areas of concern on survey after survey completed by employees? I find that when something that should be happening isn't happening regarding talent management, even though the resources are available to make it happen, one of two reasons is the cause: lack of skill or lack of will.

Let's first consider lack of will. If you're going to assume a position of influence over other people, you need to be passionate about helping them reach their potential and enjoy great success. That's non-negotiable. If a manager, human resources (HR) person, or senior leader doesn't have a desire to do everything in their power to help their employees reach their potential, they need to get out of their job immediately. It's a precious gift to be able to positively influence people, and this gift shouldn't be taken lightly. We're talking about people's lives! Some people lack the desire because they think they aren't competent at managing employees and developing their potential and, as a result, don't look forward to engaging employees. That's understandable but, more importantly, easily fixable. Which brings us to the second reason for the inability to help employees reach their potential – lack of skill.

Managing employees and developing them is a science. You need a high level of skill in several areas to be effective. Unfortunately, most managers haven't been afforded the opportunity to develop this skill set. That's a real shame but, again, easily fixable.

Whether you work for a large company or a small business, there are many mysteries, myths, gaps in knowledge or skills, and road-blocks that stand in the way of creating a great experience for the people you work with and getting the most out of them. I had the pleasure of coaching a great leader at Bank of America when I worked there as the senior vice president of leadership development. Jane Magpiong was president of the Private Bank at the time. She had a complex job with many responsibilities. She believed in helping the members of her team to become the best they could be, but lacked structure in her approach We sat down one day and discussed a more deliberate approach. In the end she said, "Okay, so basically I have five big conversations that have to happen throughout the year with my employees. I have to have the 'what I expect of you' conversation, the 'how you are doing' conversation (which is continual throughout the year), the 'how you did' conversation, the 'money' conversation, and the 'opportunities for growth' conversation, right? Right." I think this is a good framework to think about how you need to engage your employees. I've modified the words a bit, but we'll use this framework throughout the book.

It sounds funny, but this is how executives and leaders think. They think simply and obviously. They think about the business and making it successful through its employees. Unfortunately, leaders in many companies don't think as clearly or simply as Jane Magpiong about helping people be the best they can be, and with HR in the middle trying to help, often ineffectively, employees are on the receiving end of this chaos.

In this book, we're going to clear away the many mysteries, myths, gaps in knowledge or skills, and roadblocks that stand in the way of unleashing people's potential. We're going to demystify talent management for you.

Who should read this book? Managers should read it for sure. Employees should read it so they can develop a holistic view of all the talent management activities related to being developed and managed, so they can be prepared to respond to what comes their way. They will be prepared to stand up and demand competence and engagement from their managers. HR folks should read this book to challenge themselves to simplify what they're currently doing and to get the greatest impact from the combined efforts of all the various stakeholders. Senior executives should read this book so they understand what talent management activities should be going on in their organization. Senior execs should demand a high degree of talent management competence from their leaders in order to deliver consistently strong business results. Small business owners should read it because they typically lack the resources available to bigger organizations that have established talent management programs. This book offers simple practices that can be used effectively by small businesses.

Much of what we'll explore is relevant to anyone looking to get results from another person, regardless of the size of the business. For example, coaching should happen at all levels in organizations of all sizes. Letting people know what's expected of them and creating an environment where they can be successful is accomplished the same way, regardless of organizational level or size. What might change, as the company gets bigger, is the complexity of the tools and practices and the amount of resources that need to be applied to be successful.

If there are specific actions more appropriate for small businesses or large corporations, I'll note them as such. The bulk of the ideas in this book will pertain to the workplace, but you'll also find that some of them transcend the workplace and are consistent with high-performing people regardless of what they're doing.

The bottom line: this stuff really isn't hard, and it's incredibly powerful when done well. Once you fully understand it, it's quite intuitive.

I've worked in talent management for more than twenty years in global organizations. I've gathered a substantial amount of data and conducted extensive interviews with people in companies throughout the world. These big ideas have been synthesized into simple and clear approaches to each component of talent management. This book will not only help you understand how the components intersect with each other but help you to clearly understand the points of view and perspectives of the major stakeholders so you can all work toward the same goal – success.

Layout of the Book

Talent management consists of the processes, practices, and activities that are used in hiring people, determining their compensation, managing their job performance, training and developing them, and planning for replacing them should they leave or be promoted.

We'll start by looking at these different talent management activities that managers and employees engage in. Often these activities are accomplished separately, and the participants don't clearly understand how the activities relate to each other.

We'll spend most of our time exploring the two primary components of talent management – managing performance and developing employees. On the performance side, we'll go deeply into how to set good performance expectations, how to check someone's performance along the way, and how to evaluate their performance at the end of a performance cycle. On the development side, we'll look at how to help people develop in the short and long terms. We'll also take a brief look at hiring, compensation, and succession planning in the context of performance management and employee development.

There's a robust chapter on coaching and feedback. I believe this is the most effective way a manager can develop an employee. I have a real passion for coaching and feedback. It's necessary and obvious to coach. You need to do it. I'll give you some good ideas on how to do it well.

I'll close the book by showing you how to tap into people's motivation and manage their style, and I'll quickly touch base on diversity. These pieces can make or break your other talent management efforts, depending on whether they're done well or not.

Where it makes sense, I'll offer a perspective on each topic from the points of view of the CEO, the manager, the employee, and HR, as well as what their responsibilities are and where they might typically fall down in those responsibilities. But since the bulk of the responsibilities for talent management falls squarely into the manager's lap, I'll direct the tone and most of the commentary toward managers. I do strongly suggest that employees read this book and understand it from their perspective and then work to understand it from the perspective of their managers. If employees understand the possibilities available to them, they can contribute more to their own effectiveness and development. In turn, with higher-performing employees, managers can have a bigger impact and companies can see better results. It all comes back to the book's subtitle: *Unleash People's Potential to Deliver Superior Results.* That's the end game, and a good foundation of knowledge about talent management can accelerate that higher purpose.

Because there's so much research stressing the value of learning through storytelling, you'll find this book filled with stories. I've had significant positive feedback to this approach when working with individuals and with groups. The stories or examples will be about people I've worked with in my talent management roles, including as head of talent and senior vice president of leadership development, or they're from people who have shared with me their ideas and perspectives. When it's a positive story about or from someone, I've used their name. If it's not a positive story, I've eliminated their name. I've received permission to use the names and experiences I've noted in this book. I'm fortunate in that people are so willing to help others be-come better. It's an inspiration to be surrounded by great people. All you need to do is open yourself up to the people around you – there's so much to offer and be offered in all walks of life.

About the Author

I've had the pleasure of working with some great organizations and some great people. People ask where I've gotten my training. It's from working in these environments and also from my upbringing. I've worked in more than thirty countries over the last twenty years. My key strengths are in coaching and in building organizations. I've coached thousands of people around the world at all levels. I've built HR functions and I've worked with hundreds of leaders to help them build their businesses or organizations. I'm a creator. I thrive when there's a blank slate.

I'm the youngest of ten children. My parents had nine children in ten years and then six years later had me. I grew up in a micro-cosm of an organization, and the people in it were very different from each other. That's a real advantage for me when dealing with people. Being the youngest, I was afforded some extra maneuvering room (my brothers and sisters would put it differently) that allowed me the space to figure out what worked with some people and what didn't. It was a powerful learning environment.

Additionally, I'm a horsewoman. I've been riding since I was two years old. So much of what I do as a leader, as a talent developer, and as a coach I learned on the back of a horse. As someone who's a show-jumping equestrian, I need to be highly attuned to my environment because the consequences can be significant. To be successful, I need to anticipate what's coming. I must have a strong connection with the animal so we can act and think together. With that connection, most of what happens can be resolved with either a set of reins (to slow the horse down), a pair of spurs (to move the horse forward in the direc-tion you want), or a sugar cube (to send a strong message that you like what you're getting from the horse). These actions parallel working with people, and they work time and time again.

Simplicity is essential. We're too busy and frankly too tired to deal with complications. There are too many words, too many additional steps, and too many fruitless actions in life. I don't know about you, but my life is super short. Whether it be tomorrow or fifty years from now, I'm going to be dead and that freaks me out. I have a long list of things I want to accomplish, and I don't want other people's baggage to get in the way. Therefore, I'm a straight shooter. You'll always know where you stand with me. I have a zero-drama policy. Life is about winning and figuring out what you did when you lost so you can win the next time.

I like smart and hardworking people whose hearts are in the right place. I also like moderately intelligent and hardworking people whose hearts are in the right place. I also like low-intelligence and hardworking people whose hearts are in the right place. I cannot stand lazy people. I cannot stand people who expect things to come to them. I'm incredibly frustrated by people who have capability and talent but don't make the effort to develop them.

Respect is essential. I do not tolerate people who exert themselves negatively over others. I dismiss selfish people and people who have no sense of community. People deserve to be treated with respect – no one has a right to rob people of their dignity. If someone doesn't subscribe to that principle and treats people poorly, they lose the right to be in my space. I only want positive energy and positive people in my life. I will work myself to the bone for people who aren't negative.

I truly believe that most people want to be successful. I make that assumption as I enter every engagement, and I act accordingly. I also believe that many people get in the way of their own success and do the same with others. Their intentions are often good, but their impact isn't. Unfortunately, impact is what matters, so we need to pay particular attention to making sure our impact is positive.

I confess that I can be a bit difficult to manage. Tell me what you want and step aside and I'll exhaust myself in getting you the best solution. Step in my way, though, and you'll be run over. It's important to know that because I can be a tremendous powerhouse, a huge asset for you, or someone you don't want to deal with at all. It doesn't mean

I can't work with people – I do that very well. I just have high expectations of myself and the people around me and expect clarity, connectivity, and room to be successful. I'm frustrated by wasted effort and needless process. Aren't you? I hate politics – a needless drain. I will call bull on your bull and expect you to do the same with me. I've got a simple yet consistent formula that has led to tremendous success.

Promotions should be earned. Advancement and promotion should come to people who deliver excellent results and are known for developing top talent. If someone hasn't developed a successor or identified other viable options in the organization, they shouldn't be allowed to leave a position. A strong commitment to the community needs to prevail to maintain a strong pipeline of talent. Managers should be selfless. They should be servant-leaders, sharing power and putting the needs of others first. Promotions should come to people with high learning agility and a commitment to ongoing personal development so their management skill sets can grow with the ever-changing needs of the employees and the business.

These are my biases. Full disclosure. I feel strongly that I'm representative of a lot of successful people. These ways of operating have worked to help me and thousands of people around the world become successful. They've helped to clarify how to manage and develop talent. I'm writing this book to expose the poor practices going on around the world regarding talent management and, more importantly, help people understand how to do it well. There's greatness ahead of us, so let's get on with it and leave huge legacies.

The Chapter's Big Ideas

- Leading people is an honor and should be treated as such.
- If you aren't getting what you want from people, it's usually an issue of skill or will.
- All good things in an organization come from people.
- Talent management is inclusive of managing and developing employees.

- Managing employees and developing them is a science.
- Good talent management isn't hard, but it takes commitment. If it's done well, the possibilities are limitless.
- Good talent management begins with the manager.
- Managers need to have five big conversations with their employees throughout the year:
  - The "What you need to do" conversation
  - The "How you are doing" conversation
  - The "How you did" conversation
  - The "Money" conversation
  - The "How you need to grow" conversation

CHAPTER TWO

Bring It On!

DEATH BY A THOUSAND HR CUTS. Isn't that what it feels like sometimes? Every time you turn around, there's another "people" thing to do. Don't you have a job to do? Don't you have work that needs your attention rather than these activities that rob you of time and seem to add little value? Whether you're a manager, an employee, someone from the senior management team, or even someone in HR, the litany of people-related activities often seems, well, unrelated to your real work.

I'm not a fan of most HR organizations and most HR activities because, in many companies, they haven't done the right things to garner respect. They haven't done the hard but essential work of engaging the organization by managing or developing talent to enable the company's strategy. Actually, most people aren't fans of HR for various reasons. This is a broad, gross generalization, but one I've found to be true – most HR organizations aren't worth their expense. Staff in these organizations run the gamut from under-skilled to academic complicators. This is harsh, I know, but I can give you countless examples of this reality. I've been incredibly frustrated by HR organizations and their limited or negative impact on organizations (large and small) because I've seen the tremendous impact of

13

really good HR organizations and people. People who "get" the whole people-management and people-development piece have incredible power and impact. When I worked at Bank of America, there was a saying that went like this: "Finance runs the bank and HR runs Finance." That's a great snapshot of the level of influence HR had at the bank.

Great HR folks have influence because they are business people who are all about helping other business people grow their businesses. They do this by putting the best people in the most important roles. The role of HR is to enable managers. Managers are the first line of defense for all things people-related. Where there's an abundance of people or people-related activities, it makes sense that resources should be pooled and leveraged to better enable managers – this is how an HR organization is born. But first, HR people should understand the business, how the business makes money, and how to get people to contribute to their highest potential. Unfortunately, this describes too few HR organizations.

There's nothing more important than getting talent management right. This is often said but rarely understood. The number of organizations I have worked with that say this but don't realize what it fully means flabbergasts me. It's from this point of strength, getting the people piece right, that all else flows in successful companies and, actually, in most endeavors. You see it time and time again in companies that focus significant efforts on talent development.

Sonja Narcisse works for such a company, a global corporation headquartered in Stamford, Connecticut. "At Tronox, talent management connects everything we do related to our people," says Sonja, Chief Human Resources Officer. "Driving talent management is directly tied into our overall strategy for achieving business results, which makes it a fundamental pillar of Tronox. When executed consistently, we will have best-in-class people processes to benefit every employee and enable successful business results through data-driven human capital decisions. People are our most valuable asset and everyone should clearly understand why and where they fit into the organization. We achieve this through an integrated people process that consists of talent management and performance management. The effectiveness of this process directly influences our business results."

Development Dimensions International (DDI), a global company dedicated to developing talent, has extensive research that indicates that organizations with strong performance management practices are likely to outperform other organizations in areas such as productivity, profitability, revenue growth, and market value. Performance management is a key component of talent management. DDI has observed that organizations that have strong performance management methodologies and practices in place are 50 percent more likely to outperform ones that don't. That's a pretty compelling reason to engage in this work.

Before we embark on exploring each component of talent management, let's start with a simple but vital statement: Hire the best you can. It makes all the difference in the world. Be clear on what you want in an employee, and take the time to find the right one. I've been successful for two reasons. I work incredibly hard, and I surround myself with outstanding people. I once hired a training coordinator, Joyce Bachman, who had previously worked in various parts of the organization. She had a wicked tongue and was funny as hell, but I always got the straight scoop from her. She was unafraid to offer her opinion and kept us all moving forward. When I hired her, she was in her 60s. Two days after I hired her, she was on the ground in Singapore running a global program with fifty people coming in from all over the world for an important leadership development program. She was fantastic. She made the team and me better. Over-hire (hire over-qualified people) wherever you can.

Also hire for attitude. If you've worked with me in any capacity in a company, chances are you've also had the pleasure of working with a talented individual – Jackie Boucher. Jackie is the epitome of hiring for attitude. She has worked with me in three different organizations. Thank goodness. No matter what I did, where I dropped her, or what I threw at her, she navigated her way. (Speaking of dropping, I will admit that on a few trips I did threaten to leave her in some third-world country because she pushes me hard and is pretty sassy.) I had confidence in Jackie, even when she didn't have it in herself. I knew she would always manage.

We were in Mexico doing some management development work in the early 2000s. We were in a beautiful, lush resort setting in Cuernavaca with twenty leaders from a Latin American business. It was after lunch and Jackie was to kick off a short segment of the session, and I was due to conduct the rest of it. She didn't know my material well, but she'd sat in on a few sessions I'd led in the past. I said, "Jackie, I'm going to run to the restroom, so why don't you get them settled in and start your quick piece and I'll be right back." Great plan, but not what happened. The restroom was in the basement of the building. As I tried to leave the bathroom stall, I found I was locked in. The door wouldn't open. For thirty minutes I yelled as I tried to break the lock on the door. No one heard me. Because I was underground in Cuernavaca, Mexico, there was no cell-phone reception. The door went to the ceiling, and there was about a nine-inch opening at the bottom. I knew I had to go through that space. Based on the layout of the bathroom stall, the only way I could get through was to get on my hands and knees and shimmy my way out backwards. When I was halfway out I imagined what this would look like if someone walked in at that moment, and of course I started laughing and got stuck, so I had to calm down to finish extracting myself. I washed quickly, threw water on my face, and ran upstairs. Jackie was leading them through my segment, since I was now forty-five minutes late. I threw her a look as I walked in that said "Don't even ask," and she seamlessly handed the session over to me. The participants had no idea that wasn't the plan. The whole time I was in the bathroom, I wasn't worried about the participants even though Jackie had never taught that piece. (I was worried I might never be found but not worried about the participants.) That's what hiring top talent will do for you. That's what hiring for the right attitude will do for you. Once you've hired the right person you do everything in your power to make them successful, which is what the rest of this book is about.

16

Making Sense of It All at the Macro Level

Disclaimer: The rest of this chapter is a bit technical. It will address many of the HR terms you hear when dealing with people in the workplace. I'll fully define these terms for you and help you understand how they connect. When I do this with groups, people love it, but it isn't the easiest content to read about. Delving into technical aspects of talent management is something I think most managers avoid, but they end up missing the big picture and don't see how it all fits together. I promise you this is the only technical section of the book. So you have two choices. The first is to grab your nose, hold it, and jump in. Things will be much clearer if you do. The other is to put a smile on your face, commit to the idea that ignorance is bliss, and begin to delve into the major concepts of talent management described in Chapter 3.

Many business professionals don't fully understand why they should perform certain talent management practices or how they all fit together. They actually do fit together. I often engage in an exercise with groups of managers. I call it "give me all you've got." I ask them to tell me all of the HR terms they've heard of. I capture their responses on a flip chart and usually get a long list. Exhibit 2-1 shows the terms you'll usually see on that list.

There are probably some I'm missing but that's the usual set of terms managers come across in organizations, large and small, concerning HR activities. Many often execute these practices in isolation

---

- 360s
- Banding
- Bonuses
- Career Development
- Career Plans
- Coaching
- Compensation
- Competencies
- Exempt vs. Nonexempt
- Feedback
- Goals
- Hiring
- Individual Development Plans (IDPs)
- Job Evaluations
- Leadership Models
- Merit Increases
- Needs Assessments
- Peer Evaluations
- Performance Management
- Performance Reviews
- Promotions
- Ratings
- Role Profiles
- Self-Evaluations
- Stock Options
- Succession Planning
- Values

Exhibit 2-1. Most commonly heard talent management terms.

from each other, without a clear understanding of their true value or how to get the most out of them. This results in employees just doing required HR tasks or completing HR forms without knowing or caring why. Conversely, if employees clearly understood the intent of these practices, HR's and managers' efforts would be maximized and result in business benefits. For example, take performance reviews. Many managers are required to complete performance reviews. However, the vast majority of managers conduct these reviews at the last minute, pull in only small pieces of the employee's work picture, worry more about the form of the review than its content, and end up frustrating their employees with little input on their performance. They miss huge opportunities to help employees unleash their potential.

Putting the HR Term Puzzle Together – Piece by Piece

To help you avoid missing out on these opportunities, let's clear up some of the confusion about the terms and how they relate to each other. There are two major components to talent management. One is performance and the other is development.

Performance Terms

The first performance terms to consider are *performance management, role profiles,* and *goals.*

Performance Management

The end-to-end process of setting direction, giving input about how one is doing, and providing coaching, feedback, and a year-end review is called performance management. These are the primary activities related to managing performance in a given year. There may be additional activities such as a mid-year review. Some companies include all development activities under the umbrella of performance management. Other companies expand on this idea and refer to the entire cycle as the performance management and development process.

Role Profiles and Goals

Role profiles and position descriptions are generally the same thing. They describe the major duties of the role. When you create a role profile, especially one you're going to hire against or develop against, you should include the experience needed, the skills needed, and common elements that make employees derail in such roles. Anything you can do to clarify what's expected of someone in that role, generally and specifically, short term and long term, increases the odds of that person being successful in that role. Provide role clarity up front so employees can fully understand what's expected of them.

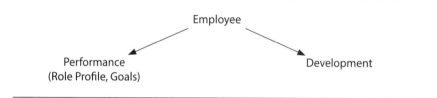

Goals tend to be different from role profiles. Goals are typically desired achievements that are separate from everyday responsibilities. They're often significant and time-bound. An example of a performance goal would be to re-engineer the mortgage workflow process to reduce time and increase customer satisfaction.

Possible inputs to goals and role profiles include the company's strategic plan, team goals, past performance plans, and business goals.

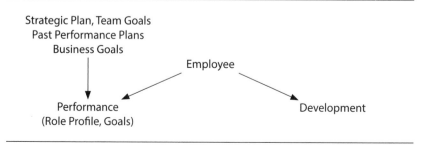

Development Terms

Employee development terms to consider include *individual development plans, career plans, career development, succession planning, competencies, values, leadership models, 360s,* and *needs assessments.*

Individual Development Plans

Individual development plans (IDPs) identify two things: the skills and capabilities employees need to develop in order to be successful in their roles and what the employees are working on in a given year that will help them to develop those skills. (As an aside - IDPs should also include components from the career plan, which looks from one to five years out in terms of where the employees expect to be in their careers as well as charting paths to get there. Integrating elements of a career plan into a 12-month individual development plan is a smart way to ensure the employee is tracking toward their longer-term goals. While a career plan is often a stand-alone plan separate from the shorter-term, 12-month-focused IDP, it's also an input to the IDP.)

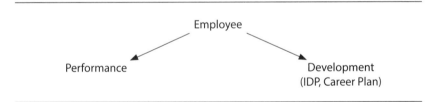

A development plan should be constructed by the employee, who has procured insights and feedback on what needs improvement or what needs to be taken to the next level. There are many possible ways in which we can develop. It's important to get data to help us decide what we should work on regarding our development over a given amount of time. These are called inputs into the development plan. Possible inputs to an IDP include components from the longer-term career plan (as we discussed briefly already), 360 results, and assessments against a competency model. Let's define some of these terms in more detail.

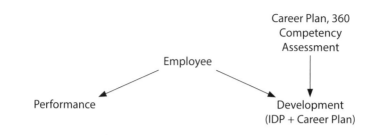

Career Plans, Career Development, and Succession Planning

Career plans are employees' longer-term perspectives on their intended career trajectories and evolution, and include lists of intentional activities and actions to support that evolution. Career plans should be broken down into manageable milestones and clearly defined dependencies. These plans should be mapped into employees' calendars in order to feed into their current-year IDPs.

Career development starts with employees asking themselves what their career goals are. In creating their career plans they should consider their company's strategic direction and how well they think they'll fit in the company in the future. If the future looks promising, employees should work with their managers to develop their capabilities so they can achieve their career goals. If not, employees should find companies that are better matches for achieving their career goals.

Career development and succession planning are two sides of the same coin – the difference is that career development is employee-driven while succession planning is company-driven. In succession planning, companies look at the strategic direction they need to take in order to survive and thrive. They then look at their talent pools and capabilities and ask, "Do we have the talent we need to meet our strategic goals and, if not, can we develop those capabilities or do we need to hire them?" Companies use succession plans to match people to future roles and to see if there are any gaps.

Competencies

Competencies are important skills, areas of knowledge, or attitudes required for success. Competency models inside organizations are the lists of agreed-upon knowledge, skills, and abilities it takes for employees to be successful. Competency models are often tailored to fit the company because different companies value different competencies. While this is the ideal scenario in my opinion, many companies use off-the-shelf models as well. There are *core* competencies (e.g., communication) that apply to everyone, *leadership* competencies (e.g., developing talent) that apply to leaders, and *functional* competencies (e.g., brand development for marketing) that make clear what excellence looks like in those functions. Competency assessments are tools used to identify the depth of capabilities of employees to perform their jobs. Sophisticated systems in organizations can link these competencies to performance appraisals, embed them in 360s, develop training curricula based on them, and develop interview questions from them for selection purposes.

Values

Companies often identify what they hold to be most important and most true. These are the company's values. These values are intended to drive the behavior of employees and guide their choices. It's important to make sure the values are not generic but truly differentiators of success for the company.

Leadership Models

Leadership models consist of a company's shared set of characteristics (skills, attitudes) they commit to because they know these characteristics will make them successful. Leadership models are powerful frameworks used by HR and managers to help them with employee selection and development, as part of performance reviews, and as the basis for 360s.

360s

360 reviews or multi-rater assessments are tools used to capture input from many stakeholders on a person's strengths and potential areas for development. The purpose is to provide multiple perspectives on an employee indicating the absence or presence of behaviors. Employees are the foremost experts on their performance. However, a single employee perspective is like looking into a mirror straight on. When you

• 360s	• Goals	• Performance
• Banding	• Hiring	Reviews
• Bonuses	• Individual Development	• Promotions
• Career Development	Plans (IDPs)	• Ratings
• Career Plans	• Job Evaluations	• Role Profiles
• Coaching	• Leadership Models	• Self-Evaluations
• Compensation	• Merit Increases	• Stock Options
• Competencies	• Needs Assessments	• Succession Planning
• Exempt vs. Nonexempt	• Peer Evaluations	• Values
• Feedback	• Performance Management	

Exhibit 2-2. Talent management terms addressed so far have been grayed-out.

go into a dressing room and try on a new shirt, it might look good in the front mirror, but awful in the side and back mirrors. You're fortunate you had multiple mirrors, but you're unhappy about it at the same time (you really liked that shirt from the front). That's true of a 360. Getting input from managers, clients, peers, and direct reports gives employees a comprehensive perspective on their work behaviors.

Needs Assessments

With good data from their employees' IDPs or succession plans, organizations can perform good needs assessments looking across IDP collectively. Companies determine what skills and areas of knowledge need to be increased to remain competitive, and then they develop plans for doing so. Needs assessments allow organizations to be intentional in their investments and plan on how they will develop their employees.

If you're keeping track, the terms grayed-out in Exhibit 2-2 are the ones we've addressed so far. Here is the puzzle as it currently stands:

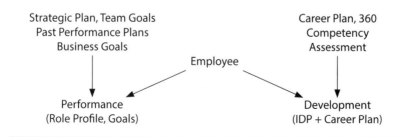

Strategic Plan, Team Goals
Past Performance Plans
Business Goals

Career Plan, 360
Competency
Assessment

Employee

Performance
(Role Profile, Goals)

Development
(IDP + Career Plan)

Other Talent Management Terms

Other important talent management terms to consider are compensation, merit increases, bonuses, stock options, banding, ratings, self-evaluations, peer evaluations, coaching, and feedback.

Compensation and Merit Increases

Compensation is generally composed of a base salary, sometimes a bonus, and, depending on the position, other perks or enticements referred to as "benefits" such as health insurance, vacations, profit sharing, etc. Typically the cost of an employee's benefits to the company is about one third of their salary. So if someone makes $50,000 a year in base salary, the company pays over $65,000 a year to employ that person, not including employment taxes. Base salaries are determined, or should be, by reviewing similar roles in similar companies in similar geographies and then deciding on a fair comparable wage based on that review. Merit increases are increases in employee compensation based on job performance (better performance, bigger increase). People aren't typically paid for progress against their development plans, rather progress against their development plans results in their acquiring new skills and knowledge, making them eligible for future promotional opportunities.

Bonuses

When people have a greater and more direct ability to influence the success of a company, a different type of compensation is often put in place – a bonus. Essentially what the employer says is: "If you're so good and can get us to be successful like you said you could by taking this important job, you need to be willing to back that up. You need to make a bet with us on the money you can earn. A portion of your pay will be at risk. If you succeed and deliver on the commitments we agree upon, you'll get this portion. If you exceed them, you'll likely get more. If you don't deliver, you could get less than this portion or even nothing." Essentially what the employee says is: "Yes, I can deliver on the commitments and I'm willing to take that bet." That's how a bonus works.

Stock Options

A person who is in a senior position and can significantly influence the company's performance or success may bet a larger portion of their overall compensation, not just on a bonus but also on stock. The assumption is that the more senior you are in an organization, the more you should be able to positively or negatively influence the stock value.

Banding

In an attempt to be fair and equitable, companies will often try to group similar jobs and similar scales of work scope and complexity in an effort to pay employees appropriately. These groups are called bands. Within a band there can be a number of types of jobs, so bands are often subdivided for better comparison. Pay bands offer organizations standardization while giving managers some discretion to reward good performance.

Ratings, Self-evaluations, and Peer Evaluations

After employees deliver their performance, a determination is made about how well they upheld their commitments. The determination of how much they did what they said they were going to do is usually classified by a rating. Typically employees reflect on their performances and do self-evaluations to determine their ratings. In some organizations, peers are asked to provide input on an employee's performance and the strength of their skills. This peer evaluation, along with the self-evaluation, should be used as input to the manager's evaluation, which is the overall final evaluation.

Coaching and Feedback

Employees and their managers must engage in ongoing conversations about the employee's performance – it's the only thing that makes this whole performance evaluation process work. Conversations include coaching (by the manager) and feedback (between the employee and the manager). Without coaching and feedback the likelihood of employee success is significantly reduced.

Putting the HR Term Puzzle Together – Almost Done

Strategic Plan, Team Goals
Past Performance Plans
Business Goals

Career Plan, 360
Competency
Assessment

Employee

Performance
(Role Profile, Goals)

Development
(IDP + Career Plan)

Did the employee do what
he or she said they were going
to do, or more or less?
(Review and Rating)
=
Compensation
(Base salary + merit
increases or at risk pay)

Coaching
&
Feedback

Skill and knowledge
development
resulting in renewed
or evolved IDP
=
Possible promotion

The terms grayed-out in Exhibit 2-3 are the ones we've addressed so far. Let's define the last few terms in the list, including *job evaluations, exempt vs. nonexempt, promotions,* and *hiring.*

Job Evaluations

Sometimes what a job was originally intended to be, as well as the compensation range for that job, seems outdated or inaccurate. Sometimes a job evolves to a point that it should be classified differently, with a different pay scale. A job evaluation is the process that makes this determination.

Exempt vs. Nonexempt

Exempt vs. nonexempt status is a U.S. governmental classification. It protects classes of employees who should be eligible for overtime. Nonexempt employees are entitled to overtime pay. The classifications are based on the type of work being done. Exempt employees are usually administrative, executive, or professional staff. Terms and strategies regarding overtime pay vary greatly from country to country.

• 360s	• Goals	• Performance
• Banding	• **Hiring**	Reviews
• Bonuses	• Individual Development	• **Promotions**
• Career Development	Plans (IDPs)	• Ratings
• Career Plans	• **Job Evaluations**	• Role Profiles
• Coaching	• Leadership Models	• Self-Evaluations
• Compensation	• Merit Increases	• Stock Options
• Competencies	• Needs Assessments	• Succession Planning
• **Exempt vs. Nonexempt**	• Peer Evaluations	• **Values**
• Feedback	• Performance Management	

Exhibit 2-3. Talent management terms addressed so far have been grayed-out.

Promotions

Promotions should be granted when the scope, scale, complexity, and sophistication of the work being done by employees has changed significantly or their capability to do this higher-level work has changed. Promotions should have nothing to do with tenure or volume – they should have to do with the employee's potential to do higher-level work.

Hiring

One element of talent management – talent acquisition – is a critical success factor. Hire for potential, hire for attitude, hire for learning agility so you can then leverage these capabilities in many different ways. As Keith Piken, a senior vice president at a major financial firm, put it, "The most important piece of advice I would have is: hire wisely and well. Developing takes time, patience, and mutual accountability. The smaller the company the more critical the hire (and the more precious your time), so view managing and development as investments in your company. Choose your investments wisely."

Not enough people understand the interconnectedness of these activities that relate to managing people and the importance of these activities to business strategy and results. Because of that lack of understanding, these elements remain just rote tasks to be performed thoughtlessly, and opportunities and potential are not fully realized. It's essential that this understanding take place. If not done correctly, in a coordinated way, these disconnected, isolated activities will be wasted effort.

In the following chapters, I'll delve into each talent management activity in great depth and provide you with appropriate context to help you more fully understand how and why to use various elements. Before we do that, however, let's take a broad look at what each stakeholder group is interested in as it relates to managing and developing people.

The Chapter's Big Ideas

- Nothing is more important in business than getting talent management right.
- Organizations with good talent management practices outperform other organizations.
- There are two major components of talent management – managing performance and developing employees.
- Talent management activities are interconnected.
- Execute talent management activities in a concerted way, otherwise they're a waste of time.
- Hire the best you can afford.
- Hire for attitude.
- Don't be afraid to over-hire for the job.

BROAD CONCEPTS OF TALENT MANAGEMENT ASSESSMENT

On a scale of 1 to 10, with 1 being not at all and 10 being at an industry standard level, rate your organization on the following questions:

	LOW 1 2 3 4 5 6 7 8 HIGH 9 10
1. How well do your employees understand the interrelated elements of talent management?	☐ ☐ ☐ ☐ ☐ ☐ ☐ ☐ ☐ ☐
2. How clearly understood is your company's compensation system?	☐ ☐ ☐ ☐ ☐ ☐ ☐ ☐ ☐ ☐
3. Is your HR organization valued?	☐ ☐ ☐ ☐ ☐ ☐ ☐ ☐ ☐ ☐
4. Do new hires receive a quality education relating to talent management activities?	☐ ☐ ☐ ☐ ☐ ☐ ☐ ☐ ☐ ☐
5. Are HR practices fair and equitably applied to all?	☐ ☐ ☐ ☐ ☐ ☐ ☐ ☐ ☐ ☐
6. Does your company aggressively over-hire where possible to bring top talent into the pipeline?	☐ ☐ ☐ ☐ ☐ ☐ ☐ ☐ ☐ ☐
7. Are your HR practices reliable, repeated, and consistent?	☐ ☐ ☐ ☐ ☐ ☐ ☐ ☐ ☐ ☐
8. Are managers, HR, employees, and senior management on the same page regarding talent management?	☐ ☐ ☐ ☐ ☐ ☐ ☐ ☐ ☐ ☐
9. Are managers highly skilled and do they assume complete responsibility for successfully managing the talent?	☐ ☐ ☐ ☐ ☐ ☐ ☐ ☐ ☐ ☐
10. Are competencies linked to a 360, which is linked to a performance plan, which is linked to compensation for the employees?	☐ ☐ ☐ ☐ ☐ ☐ ☐ ☐ ☐ ☐
11. Are there stellar coaches in the organization?	☐ ☐ ☐ ☐ ☐ ☐ ☐ ☐ ☐ ☐
12. Are promotions granted based on delivering excellent results and developing top talent?	☐ ☐ ☐ ☐ ☐ ☐ ☐ ☐ ☐ ☐

BROAD CONCEPTS OF TALENT MANAGEMENT ACTION STEPS

For anything you rated less than 9, what are you going to do about it?

Question #	Actions to Take	Timeframe	People to Involve

CHAPTER THREE

Stakeholder Points of View

ALMOST EVERYONE IN YOUR COMPANY sees a piece of the puzzle when it comes to managing and developing employees, but only a few see the whole puzzle. One of the challenges of talent management is that the people engaging in it view things based only on *their* point of view. This myopia can cause breakdowns in the process. People often shy away from talent management activities because they view them as separate from the important work of the business and trivialize them as "just another thing we have to do." Or sometimes these activities just seem overwhelming. Further complicating matters, most people don't understand how to do them well and, as a result, many are often fearful of these activities. Add company culture and dynamics to the mix and employees don't trust talent management activities and often disengage. If they do engage, and these challenges are still present, they often engage only superficially. But with a robust and comprehensive understanding of talent management from all parties involved, a better end result should occur (if the right levels of skill and commitment are also present).

From the CEO's and Senior Leader's POV

Many CEOs and senior leaders view talent management in terms of cost, and they're mostly concerned with its return on investment. For them, it's all about business results, the bottom line. It's particularly true if they're in a publicly traded company. They have a fiduciary responsibility to deliver superior business results. So, with this as their perspective, their focus is usually: how does talent management add value? Key questions they'll ask are: Do we really need to do it? What's the least amount of time and attention we can afford it and still make it worth our effort? These are great questions, ones that other stakeholders should be asking as well.

I used to work with a CEO in a company that was cash rich at the time. He would say, "The cash you're talking about using for talent management is sitting and earning 9 percent right now. It's doing that without us doing anything. So, convince me that it's worth pulling it out of that nearly sure thing to put into this project, and tell me how you're going to return more than 9 percent on that investment." That's how CEOs think, and rightfully so. But is this how managers, HR folks, and employees think when trying to get senior leaders on board when it comes to investing in people? Including spending time on talent management practices and processes? Most managers, HR folks, and employees don't think this way, nor do they present good business cases to substantiate their ideas. Therefore, most senior leaders aren't feeling the love for talent management that they could be. I happen to agree very much with the CEO's perspective. If you aren't going to get a big return in the short or long term, don't do it. (The fact that different people define long term differently adds to the challenge.) But, if you have the potential to get a big return (and have a great business case justifying this return), well then, not only should you do it but you should make sure you do it incredibly well.

A focus on people has always been necessary for success, but it's never received more attention than it does today. There's tremendous pressure coming from a variety of sources – external regulatory agencies, the competitive marketplace, the demands of a global economy, the speed of technology and information, a shrinking and aging workforce, company boards of directors – all of which makes a focus on talent essential. Increasing productivity, return-on-investment, shareholder value, and employee satisfaction and engagement are no longer an option but necessary for success.

Therefore the majority of the senior leadership team's focus should be on talent management. They should be running the business by enabling and developing great leaders. Someone I previously worked with at a consumer goods company put it well: "Judge your success as a leader by the success of your people. And don't underestimate the importance of your role in preparing them for the future – including to one day take on your role." For many senior leaders, though, talent management isn't the focus. They often lack the knowledge they need to manage talent well. And for those who are insecure, developing their successors is a tough concept to deal with. They might not engage in the right talent management practices for personal reasons as well as lack of knowledge. For many senior leaders in most organizations there's a significant need for improvement.

From the Manager's POV

Some managers view talent management as an important part of their jobs, but many managers are unskilled at it. This is a harsh and unflattering statement but it's true. Managers (and adults in general) want to be viewed as competent. They often reach the status of "manager" because they were at the top of their function delivering good functional results, so they were promoted. On Friday they were promoted and on Monday they come to work, they're the manager, and they're expected to continue to deliver good results. What happened over the weekend to make them an effective manager, a good leader? Did they go to a revival meeting in the woods, get clunked on the head, shout, "I believe," and become enlightened? Of course not! However, when employees step into manager roles, they're often given little direction and little time to learn the job, but they're expected to be good managers from the get-go. This practice is common throughout the world. And super stupid.

Leading people is a discipline. The scenario above is equivalent to saying that on Friday you're a marketing person and on Monday you need to be an industrial engineer. Or on Friday you speak Spanish and on Monday you need to speak Mandarin. We wouldn't think of asking anyone to do these things. Yet the lack of respect often shown to new managers – by those responsible for their promotions who don't seem to realize the significant difference between doing the work and leading others who are doing the work – shows up in the low talent management skill set seen in managers throughout the world.

When faced with talent management activities, managers often don't do them or do them at a superficial level, all the while experiencing a high level of anxiety. You might occasionally have a manager who takes it upon himself or herself to read, go to training, and get a mentor in order to be a better manager. But they're the rare exceptions. Managers try to juggle a host of activities. And as the talent management activities come down the pike, they are pressured to quickly execute them and get them off their desk rather than to intelligently and thoughtfully utilize them to improve the business. It's no surprise then that time and time again managers are rated poorly in surveys by their employees.

As a respected peer of mine, Dave Mitchell, says, "Tools and processes are only as good as the people implementing and facilitating them." Dave is the CEO of The Leadership Difference, and he's helped many organizations by educating their leaders on how to raise their game. He's seen the fallout on the employee side when leaders don't learn.

There's a good book you should read called *The Leadership Pipeline* by Ram Charan, Steve Drotter, and Jim Noel. They expertly explain an important concept: As you rise in the organizational hierarchy, you need to change what you value, your skill set, and what you spend your time on in order to be effective at the next level. What often happens is that if new managers don't have the skills needed to manage, they remain or go back to "doing" the work. They even take pride in themselves for "being in the trenches" or "not asking their team to do something they aren't willing to do." Well, that's an admirable sentiment but a misplaced one. If a manager is doing the work of his or her employees, then the manager is just an overpaid individual contributor. It's a shame. And it can be easily fixed with the right commitment, instruction, practice, and coaching.

From HR's POV

You will often find that organizations follow one of two HR models. One is a generalist model in which the HR practitioners have a broad set of responsibilities – they do a little bit of everything. The other is a specialist model in which the HR practitioners are skilled in specific areas of human resource management – similar work is grouped and done by specialists. Both models provide challenges in terms of HR being a good partner to managers regarding talent management. The first and foremost challenge is lack of resources. Good talent management work takes time, money, and skilled people. In my twenty-plus years of working in corporations around the world, I've never seen an over-resourced HR function. I've seen a well-resourced HR function on a few occasions, but that was the exception. This reality often creates a "fire-fighting" approach to doing talent management work, focusing on taking care of short-term challenges rather than developing long-term solutions that will lead to superior business success.

Take generalists, for example. In a true generalist model, about 20 percent of an HR generalist's time should be spent on training. How many generalists do you know who train or do some training-related activity one full day every week? As for HR specialists, a compensation specialist for example, they often don't fully understand the end-to-end picture of the business, creating solutions to talent management challenges that are often not the best solutions for the business.

Add to this the fact that HR folks in general are often removed from knowing and understanding the intricacies of the business; the result is under-resourced HR folks who are isolated in their perspective. Ask them to implement or support the implementation of talent management activities (in large volumes) and you'll find that most HR folks will emphasize the task aspect of the work – getting the forms filled out – rather than putting in the correct thought and effort needed to manage these activities in order to realize the best return for the business. The final challenge is the fact that most HR people report into the line of business they support. This is the proverbial fox guarding the hen house. How are these folks supposed to push hard on the business to do the tough but relevant and critical work regarding people if their promotions, pay, bonuses, etc. are being determined by these same people? So from HR's point of view, talent management gets to be mostly about moving the workflow forward.

From the Employee's POV

Employees view talent management activities typically in one of two ways based on past experience. If they have been part of a system with capable managers and HR partners, they view these activities in terms of the benefits they can get out of them. They appreciate the value of talent management when it's done well (which means they're getting the support they need to be the best they can be at what they do). If employees have struggled or have been negatively impacted by these activities in the past, they too often see it as a challenge or a waste of time. Most organizations don't engage employees in the activities that would most benefit them. If managers or HR do engage employees, it's often using a hit and run approach, where employees are asked for information but then nothing is done with it. Or every year or so a new talent management program is introduced that has little or no staying power, no hint as to why it's important to the company's strategy, and no clear benefit to the employees. It's just the "flavor of the month." Employees get suspicious of such activities and find it hard to be engaged and honest with those in charge of the activities.

On the flip side, employees are typically interested in good and productive talent management activities. They want good direction.

They want insight on how they're doing in their jobs. They want to know what they need to learn and how to go about learning. They want to know how they can get to the next level. But they're often afraid to ask about these issues, and if they do ask and are met with resistance (as they often are), they tend to not ask again. I could name right now over 200 smart, engaged, hard-working people who would be too afraid to approach their managers with questions about talent management activities. There are some exceptions, but even hard-charging folks sometimes find it difficult to care about talent management when their managers are incompetent.

At one company, I worked with a promising young lawyer in a leadership development program. She was opinionated and vocal. She was smart and interested in her development. She was also African American. Her manager had no clue how to manage her. She would push him for feedback, and the things he said were so archaic that we had to laugh about them. For example, one time he told her she needed to be less vocal because she was intimidating people, especially being a black woman. In addition to being the chief talent officer, I was also head of diversity and I nearly died. He was a lawyer in the company as well! Ultimately she had to work around him to be considered for any development, while I worked with *his* manager (the general counsel) on his development. Fortunately the general counsel was a good manager who was interested in development and willing to address the problem head on. The young lawyer and I understood what we were dealing with and shook our heads about the incredible ignorance that existed in the management ranks. We worked to correct her issues and I worked to correct his issues. Unfortunately, this is only one example of what goes on regularly around the world. The need for employee development is intuitive and obvious. The fact that it's often not done or done badly makes me want to climb to the top of my laundry pile and throw myself off. And that's a real threat.

I'm admittedly harsh when discussing the level of competence of HR and managers regarding talent management. Unfortunately it's the reality around the world. It's foolish and unnecessary. So let's change it and make a new reality. Using all we've discussed as our foundation, let's get started pulling apart the major concepts of talent management, starting with the idea that a manager needs to have five big conversations:

- The "What you need to do" conversation
- The "How you are doing" conversation (this one should happen often throughout the year)
- The "How you did" conversation
- The "Money" conversation
- The "How you need to grow" conversation

Let's start with the "What you need to do" conversation, which is largely about setting good performance expectations.

The Chapter's Big Ideas

- Talent management activities should be viewed from all perspectives – employees, managers, HR, and CEOs and senior leaders – to get the best results.
- You get disconnected results when stakeholders only focus on how they see things and don't consider the views and needs of other stakeholders.
- Without a comprehensive view of talent management activities as well as a concerted effort at implementing them, the activities can be easily trivialized and become just meaningless tasks, not worth the effort.
- People are fearful of talent management activities they don't understand and often disengage from them.
- CEOs and senior leaders are primarily concerned with the value that talent management activities add to the business.
- Managers, employees, and HR should focus on the business as if they were the CEO.

- People promoted to management on Friday don't become competent by Monday.

- Getting the people piece right is a necessary condition for survival in today's business world.

- Senior leaders need to develop strong talent management skills and be highly engaged in talent management activities in order to be successful and productive.

- Managers worldwide don't have the skill sets they need to successfully manage and develop their teams.

- Employees are leery of talent management activities that have a "flavor of the month" taste to them.

- Managers are the most influential parties when it comes to creating great talent management practices and outcomes.

- Employees want good direction and want to be successful.

STAKEHOLDERS ASSESSMENT

On a scale of 1 to 10, with 1 being not at all and 10 being at an industry standard level, rate your organization on the following questions:

	LOW 1 2 3 4 5 6 7 8	HIGH 9 10
1. How well do all stakeholders (senior execs, HR, managers, employees) understand and engage in talent management activities?	☐ ☐ ☐ ☐ ☐ ☐ ☐ ☐	☐ ☐
2. To what degree do senior managers hold managers accountable for highly effective talent management practices?	☐ ☐ ☐ ☐ ☐ ☐ ☐ ☐	☐ ☐
3. How different and significant do managers see their role as manager compared to their previous functional role?	☐ ☐ ☐ ☐ ☐ ☐ ☐ ☐	☐ ☐
4. How much does HR drive talent management activities from a business mindset rather than an activity mindset?	☐ ☐ ☐ ☐ ☐ ☐ ☐ ☐	☐ ☐
5. How informed are employees on the entire talent management and development cycle and how each piece interrelates with the others?	☐ ☐ ☐ ☐ ☐ ☐ ☐ ☐	☐ ☐
6. How comprehensive are the "What you need to do" conversations?	☐ ☐ ☐ ☐ ☐ ☐ ☐ ☐	☐ ☐
7. How comprehensive are the "How you are doing" conversations?	☐ ☐ ☐ ☐ ☐ ☐ ☐ ☐	☐ ☐
8. How easy are the "How you did" conversations based on the work done in setting goals and tracking performance through the year?	☐ ☐ ☐ ☐ ☐ ☐ ☐ ☐	☐ ☐
9. How consistent, reliable, and understandable are the elements of the "Money" conversations?	☐ ☐ ☐ ☐ ☐ ☐ ☐ ☐	☐ ☐
10. How needed and important are the "How you need to grow" conversations?	☐ ☐ ☐ ☐ ☐ ☐ ☐ ☐	☐ ☐

STAKEHOLDERS ACTION STEPS

For anything you rated less than 9, what are you going to do about it?

Question #	Actions to Take	Timeframe	People to Involve

PART II

Managing Performance

CHAPTER FOUR

The "What You Need To Do" Conversation

T HE "WHAT YOU NEED TO DO" CONVERSATION is all about setting performance expectations or goals. It's part of the performance management process. What's shocking about this talent management topic is that these expectations often aren't set well, are often set late, or aren't set at all in many organizations.

Companies have the most success when their employees clearly understand their roles and responsibilities and do so in the context of the big picture. This makes sense, right? I'm a huge fan of helping people be successful. It's a bias of mine. When in doubt, help people be successful. Everyone wins with that. It doesn't mean that you do their job or figure things out for them. What it means is that you tell them what success looks like and help them achieve it. Would you get into a car without telling the driver where they need to go and how to get there? Of course you wouldn't. The equivalent of that is done in the workplace throughout the world day in and day out.

Steve Clark, who has been a senior HR executive at several well-known organizations, including the 2002 Salt Lake City Olympics, will tell you that "the performance management process is difficult for managers. It's difficult to be objective and honest. Most prefer to tell everyone they are doing okay (or great). When this happens, the process is a massive waste of time and company resources. If the process is taken seriously and done with discipline from top to bottom, it will focus the organization on what matters with meaningful and relevant employee objectives, help separate the good from the great, and allow the organization to reward, recognize, and retain the best while upgrading where needed each year."

I've worked with thousands of people in over thirty countries. More than 50 percent of those I've worked with had no performance expectations or goals, about 20 percent had them and they were good ones, and 30 percent had some that were useless for one reason or another. Think about that. More than half of the people I've worked with didn't have established performance expectations. Isn't that insane? If you ask employees, they would tell you it is indeed.

Managers offer many reasons for not setting performance expectations:

- Not enough time
- Not given expectations from the manager one level above them
- Things can change
- Hard to change them once given
- Not good at it
- No one is making them do it
- People don't like to be boxed in

Kevin Wilde, the Chief Learning Officer at General Mills, will tell you, "Performance management – it's always too complex. It's a compromise between two very different objectives – evaluate vs. inspire."

Steve and Kevin are right. Setting performance expectations can be challenging, but it's essential. The reasons it isn't being done probably have some validity, but they're really just excuses. It doesn't matter why performance expectations aren't being set.

Here's the demystification – SET THEM. You don't need to read the rest of the chapter if you get that message. The rest of the chapter will give you some hows and whys, but at the end of the day the big message is – SET THEM. The succinctness is not to downplay the message – it's to emphasize the enormity and clarity of the message. It's a consequential message!

Davide Paganoni, a business unit leader at Alexion, is adamant about keeping the message simple so managers actually use their process. "Performance management needs to be just-in-time. A delay in setting objectives and roles … they lose credibility and the tool/process becomes only homework without real value. In general all the tools that are too complex, with many different steps, are in my experience at high risk of failure. It's better to focus on single, simple, and practical steps."

Before we go further, a quick note about terminology. I use the following terms interchangeably: goals, performance expectations, key priorities, and objectives. Most employees don't care about the finer points that may distinguish one of these terms from another. What's important is that we clearly understand what's required of employees in their jobs over a given amount of time.

Performance Expectations and Strategic Direction

Follow these suggestions to help make setting performance expectations easier and make your organization's vision a reality:

1. Start with the strategic direction of the business and have performance goals flow from there.

2. Use measures to ensure you get where you want to go.

3. Get buy-in from your customers and suppliers.

4. Create an upside for achieving goals and a downside for not achieving them.

5. Work your plan, and if things change, rework it.

6. Be public about your work and commitments.

7. Keep it simple.

TIP #1

Start with the strategic direction of the business and have performance goals flow from there.

Several years ago I was working as the senior vice president of leadership development at Bank of America when Brian Moynihan was heading up the Global Wealth business before he became CEO. Brian had a true vision for the organization. He wanted a consistent look, feel, and experience for the client. In his view, every Starbucks you walk into creates a similar experience for the consumer. He called this the "Branded Client Experience" and thought that clients of the bank were also owed this highly consistent experience. To operationalize this belief, we brought 600 of his top leaders in that multi-billion-dollar business to a meeting in Florida. In addition to driving key messages during the week, we orchestrated market visits in which teams had to travel to various places such as Starbucks, certain retail operations, and other financial institutions to experience and observe the "Branded Client Experience." It was very powerful. When we brought everyone back to the larger meeting, groups brainstormed about what needed to be done to create this experience for Global Wealth clients. Those ideas were translated into deliverables that were eventually captured on individual performance plans as performance goals. It's a terrific example of how to take a company priority and make it real for each employee so that it can be achieved.

Starting with the company's strategic direction and cascading it throughout the company isn't a new concept. There's a lot written on the subject. What usually happens, however, is that the process breaks down somewhere in the middle. Often the company's strategic direction doesn't get cascaded past the first few top layers of the organization. Sometimes it does and the process works. If senior leaders have done a good job in laying out the company's strategy, it's likely that the next level down will have translated it into the business unit priorities. Then these next-level leaders often have clearly established performance expectations that relate to the company's strategic direction. My experience in working with a number of companies, however, is that it's a crapshoot as to whether strategic direction gets translated below the business unit level.

The cascade should include not only strategic priorities but also important values and competencies. When everyone in the company knows the values of the organization and understands how to act accordingly, the company's character is defined and stands for something. Sometimes, as with strategic direction, company values haven't been cascaded throughout the company. A few years ago I was at a competition with my daughter, Hannah. (My son Michael, 19, and daughter Hannah, 16, are training hard to become two of the top show jumping equestrians in the world.) Gift bags were given to the competitors. In each gift bag there was a rabbit's foot. My daughter pulled it out and asked, "Is this a real rabbit's foot?" I said, "No. There's no way that would be a real rabbit's foot! C'mon, the sponsor's whole purpose is to protect animals, especially from cruel practices. They'd never allow that." A few days after we got home from this event, a letter arrived in the mail. The letter apologized for a real rabbit's foot being in the gift bag. Seriously? I was blown away by this mistake. Who authorized that? How can everyone in that organization not understand his or her role in fulfilling the organization's purpose? But it happens often at lower levels in organizations where the company's values haven't been cascaded. Clearly the person filling these bags didn't get the memo. (The next year they put knives in the gift bags. They have more work to do.)

Managers need to feel personally accountable for driving strategic intent throughout the organization. It should be the responsibility of every manager to insist on knowing the performance expectations and goals of *their* manager. It should also be that manager's responsibility to translate those goals into relevant key priorities for the employees in the workgroup or function who report to him or her. I often run workshops that focus on teaching people how to write good goals and establish key priorities for their teams. The attendees are tasked to bring a list of their manager's goals to the workshop. When it comes time to draft their own goals, and I direct them to take out the list of their manager's goals, more than half don't have them. Of those who don't have them, most were hesitant to ask their manager for them. I find that fascinating. People would rather be confused, set inappropriate goals, have anxiety around ambiguity, or risk not being successful rather than have a constructive conversation with their manager about what the manager's goals are. It's indicative of how deeply fear runs in organizations. And it should serve notice to all the managers reading this book: don't make your employees come to you for a list of your goals – roll them out to your employees yourself.

It's just good business sense to work hard at cascading strategic intent. The power that comes to employees when they clearly understand not only what they need to deliver but also how they fit into the big picture of the company is significant. A friend of mine from college, Tony Lowe, worked in several different industries until he built his own company, Shoreline Services. His experience is similar to that of others in terms of the positive return he gets when he invests the time to educate his employees about what's important. "The employees seem to rely on the 'big picture' goals when they are placed in a situation with our customers. For example: we tell our employees that we want to provide the best possible service in our industry. Many times (for the employee and the customer) 'the best possible service' means same-day service. I have found that employees will do anything possible to deliver. That's a competitive advantage for us and it's essential they are clear about their responsibility in making this happen." Without this clarity, the employees would be left to their own devices and might make decisions inconsistent with strategic intent.

That cascading strategic intent makes good business sense is true across the globe. My colleagues in Europe have been ahead of the curve in aligning and cascading key strategic priorities. Jacques Pradels started as a commercial director, became the president of a consumer products business in France, and eventually had his responsibilities expanded to run a region. As his role became more complex and his scope wider, he had to lean on new approaches to ensure everyone under his responsibility was aligned with the business strategy. Jacques was being held to deliver one number by the CEO, one set of outputs for his region. His individual country business units needed to deliver on their numbers so they rolled up to Jacques' overall number. His approach, which he refers to as management by objective, was instrumental in his success in this new role. "The concept is to fix clear goals and KPIs (key performance indicators), from the top to the bottom, focused on the company targets and vision. The efficiency comes from the transparency, the clarity, and the focus. It is about understanding the gap and deciding concrete actions and timings to fill this gap, both through individual and collective performance. This is a strong tool to drive results, ownership, and meritocracies." This concept of rolling a responsibility up and down the organization is essential to achieving desired overall business results.

Setting individual performance expectations is important for all of the reasons we've discussed. It's ultimately important so the company can fulfill its commitments. Let's take Hasbro, for example. In the mid-1990s Mattel tried to acquire Hasbro. Hasbro avoided that takeover, but the attempt prompted a much tighter focus on business results. Alan Hassenfeld as Chairman and then Al Verrecchia as CEO embarked on an aggressive approach to delivering results. One of the key components of that approach was to drive performance accountabilities throughout the organization. If Al Verrecchia gave a number to the Toy Group on what they needed to deliver, he expected that number to be delivered. That meant the numbers for Girls Toys plus Boys Toys plus the other toy divisions had to add up to the overall Toy Group number. That meant, for Boys Toys for example, the numbers for the Batman product line plus the Supersoaker product line plus the Nerf product line, etc., had to add up to the Boys Toys number. That meant the folks working on the Nerf product line each had to deliver their piece – marketers, designers, engineers, packaging folks, etc. The head of the marketing team for Nerf had to ensure all of the people working on that team were clear about what they had to deliver and their roles in delivering it. For example, a marketing manager might be responsible for shooting three commercials and launching eight new products as their part in delivering the marketing piece.

Let's look at this example backwards. Let's say the marketing managers on the Nerf team didn't deliver because the commercials weren't made and the promotions weren't finished. Consequently, the marketing team didn't complete the work they needed to market Nerf as planned, so the Nerf team would likely not make their number. If the Nerf team didn't make their number, the Boys Toys team might not make their number depending on how big a piece of the business Nerf was at the time. If Boys Toys didn't make their number, again depending on what percentage that business was of the overall business, Hasbro might have fallen short of Al and Alan's commitments or Wall Street's expectations. If that happened, the stock price could fall. If either Girls Toys or Games didn't meet their numbers, you could see how Hasbro could have under-performed. But more importantly, you can see how companies will perform well if all of the commitments of all the business lines and divisions and departments are known throughout the organization and employees understand how their work interrelates to the other parts of the company.

Three reasons consistently show up in most surveys as to why people leave companies – poor relationships with their managers, lack of development, and lack of clarity on how they contribute to the company's overall success. These three problems are solvable, and the last one is easily solved by simply setting good performance expectations that are cascaded from the company's strategic direction.

The Manager's Responsibilities

Let's assume you're the head of the soccer equipment business at a top sporting goods company that has a corporate business priority to be in the first or second leadership spot in the market for each major category. As the head of this business line, you would need to determine your market position and consider what you'd need to do to keep or improve your position. As the leader of this team, you'd need to ensure, as a team, you were clear about what your ultimate goal was and what you needed to do together to reach it. You'd then need to work with marketing, product development, sales, manufacturing, finance, etc. to determine what each function would be responsible to do to deliver on this goal. Each functional head would then need to take their responsibilities and further break them down so, right down to the line employee, everyone was clear about what was expected of them.

This may seem complicated but it really isn't. The CEO and senior leadership team set the strategic direction, answering the question: What do we need to deliver next year in order to reach our goals? Once the senior leadership team has answered that question and made the answer known throughout the organization, managers should ask themselves:

- What can we do in our organization to ensure we achieve our strategic priorities?

- What strategic relationships are necessary for us to achieve these priorities?

- What's the right level of accountability and responsibility for the leaders on my team to achieve these priorities?

- If we each meet our responsibilities, will the collective results roll up and help the company achieve its strategic priorities?

- What might hold us back from achieving the priorities – absence of the right talent, gaps in skill, inadequate funding, or conflicting priorities?

Let's say your senior leadership team hasn't seen the light, and they haven't done a good job of setting the strategic direction for your organization. Does that get you, a manager, off the hook for setting performance expectations for your work group? The answer is a big NO! It doesn't matter what anyone else has or hasn't done. At the end of the day, you take home a paycheck as a manager. That means you need to step up and manage. The people who work for you deserve clarity about what they should be working on, and they need to get that clarity from you. It's unfortunate if your senior leadership team hasn't been clear about the strategic direction of the company. It just means you'll need to work harder. What I described previously was a top-down approach to cascading strategic priorities. If you don't get what you need from the top, you may need to be creative and leverage other people in your organization to get whatever input you can about the company's strategic direction. (It's actually a powerful way to establish engagement and accountability with your team at the same time.) For example, here's how I worked with my teams in the past:

- I had a well-defined process for setting performance expectations that I used in all of the companies where I worked.

- I would ask my customers early on what was important to them for the next year. I would look at their business objectives and see where the gaps were on the people side in terms of helping them meet these objectives.

- I would ask my leader what he was being held accountable for.

- I would talk with our CEO, listen to the board of directors, and look at things such as employee survey results to determine key messages or trends. (I would frequently assign these responsibilities to members of my team, dividing them into two sets: having conversations and doing research.)

- I would then host a strategic planning brainstorming session with my team.

  - We would review the inputs and data.

  - We would do a brain dump on all of the things that could or should vie for our attention over the next year.

  - We would put a high, medium, or low rating next to each item once the brainstorming was completed.

  - The session usually ran about four hours.

  - I would take the summary to my customers and present to them what we thought should be our priorities. The list contained mostly high priorities with a few mediums, and any low priority item was taken off the list. I would capture their input and modify the list if necessary.

- Once the list was finalized, I would bring it back to my team and we would have another brainstorming session. In that session we would determine major milestones, including dependencies and who on the team would be responsible for which major deliverables. I often left the responsibility of deliverables assignment up to the team, allowing for preferences, strengths, or areas people wanted to stretch or develop. I trusted my team to do the right thing. They worked for me because they wanted to be challenged and grow, and they knew I would help them. By choosing their areas of concentration and deliverables and negotiating with each other on priorities, they established ownership and, in turn, set direction for their careers. It's basic human nature to put more effort into the things that interest you or hold value for you for whatever reason. Managers are smart to capitalize on that.

- My team would translate these key priorities into individual objectives for the next year. I would send a final copy of the team's objectives and commitments to the senior leadership team since our work was high profile for the organization, to the HR board (the HR leadership team for the company) so they could communicate with their business and make their own plans, and to my leader to make sure everyone was on the same page. It was such a valued process that people on my team would ask when we were going to do our strategic planning brainstorming for next year ... was it on the calendar yet?

Regardless of where you start your process for setting performance expectations, it's important that you finish with every person in the organization clearly understanding the company's strategic direction and understanding his or her part in meeting strategic objectives.

TIP #2

Use measures to ensure you get where you want to go.

The idea of setting a goal without a measure seems a bit crazy to me. You wouldn't set a goal of running twenty miles without a mechanism for measuring distance to see how well you're doing in reaching that goal. But so many times we give directions without clearly defining what we're looking for – the measure – which is what you use to determine whether the goal was met.

When I tell my daughter to clean her room, and I go back in and take a look, it's often not close to what I had in mind. I didn't expect to see small pieces of paper on the floor, things stuffed under her bed, clothes piled on a chair. (I should have, based on living with this precious but messy child her whole life.) Shame on me. She executed according to what she thought was "good enough," and I didn't communicate the specificity of what I wanted. On round two, I said "Good start. Now, make sure, as you finish, that there's no trash or anything on the floor like that, or that, or that. Make sure all your clothes are put away or hung up. I don't want to see clutter on your desk or stuffed under your bed. Everything should be in its proper place." I didn't get a resounding "thank you" from her for clarifying my expectations by telling her what I was going to measure, but I was satisfied knowing I had a better chance of getting the results I wanted the next time. (And if I didn't, she was toast, and I communicated that too.) Yet, in the future I need to start with this level of precision so she can spend less time and I can reduce frustration for both of us about what I want.

This example sounds simple, but this point is simple. Tell people what you want and exactly what it looks like when it's delivered so they can be successful in delivering it. Although it should be simple to do right, setting goals is unfortunately often done without providing measures. Based on my conversations with employees, goal setting is a practice that needs much improvement around the world.

Whenever you hear about setting goals, you're bound to hear the SMART acronym. Depending on where you come from, the letters in the acronym can stand for different, somewhat related, words. But whatever words you use, the results of being SMART in setting your goals are good, clearly defined goals:

S = specific, significant, stretching

M = measurable, meaningful, motivational

A = agreed upon, attainable, achievable, acceptable, action-oriented

R = realistic, relevant, reasonable, rewarding, results-oriented

T = time-based, time-bound, timely, tangible, traceable

Certainly your goals need to be specific and, as we just discussed, measurable. Everyone involved (you, your manager, their manager) should agree upon these goals, which have to be realistically attainable. And you should have a time frame attached to them, so you know how much time you have to reach the goals. Ensuring your goals have these elements increases the likelihood of your success in achieving them and serves to clear up any ambiguity surrounding the goal.

The most important factor in goal setting, however, is the measure. This piece is vital. It's also the piece that's most often overlooked. People get a bit squeamish about measures for a variety of reasons:

- It takes *resources* to track and utilize some measures.
- People think that *complicated measures* are the only good measures.
- Measures clearly establish *accountability.*
- People *lack competence* in developing measures and consequently are afraid they might pick the wrong ones.

Resources
It takes effort to measure. Some organizations have whole functions that are dedicated to measuring and tracking. The danger around lack of resources to measure appropriately is that people sometimes pick measures not because the measure will provide them with the best information about what they want to know but because it's readily

available. For example, if you're interested in improving employee engagement and you're already measuring turnover, you might decide to use turnover as a measure of employee engagement. But you need to ask yourself: Is turnover the best measure to use? Maybe. Not sure. How do you know how engaged your employees are? Perhaps scores on an employee survey would provide better information than turnover statistics to help explain why people leave the company. It may be for other reasons other than engagement, like low pay. Be vigilant on using the right measure.

Complicated Measures

Sometimes a complicated situation needs a complicated assessment. When you're doing something highly sophisticated, you may need a sophisticated measure to give you insight. Most times, however, this isn't the case. Take the example above: employee engagement. The best measure to use is improvement in engagement scores based on employee survey results. You may shy away from using this measure if you don't have past survey results to compare to because you can't measure improvement. Sometimes you need a start-up measure to get you going. Maybe your first-year measure needs to be survey participation and not improvement in engagement, and you can make intelligent inferences from that less-than-ideal information the first year.

Sears and Mobil had great success in the 90s using the Balanced Scorecard approach to measurement. With keen precision in their measures, they were actually able to determine what every dollar spent on employee development netted in terms of increase in employee engagement scores and, in turn, what that translated to in terms of customer satisfaction scores. Sometimes really good data and measures can drive innovative thinking and better decisions. I worked with a guy who was highly skilled at using models to predict the number of executives who would be needed at various levels, based on current growth rates. He was a genius. His work was used directly in developing hiring plans, succession plans, and talent development plans. So although I'm not a fan of using complicated measures, they do have a place if they're used correctly.

To figure out how complicated your measure needs to be, you need to think in terms of "how much": What do you need to know to make sure the end result is *enough* to get you where you want to be? How much is enough? For example, let's say you have a performance expectation of improving customer satisfaction. If your manager is expecting a 20 percent improvement in customer satisfaction scores, and you're thinking more in the 5 percent range, and you don't plan to use scores but rather rely on how things "feel," you've got a major disconnect. This type of disconnect happens quite often because the specifics of "how much" aren't discussed and agreed upon. If you can use a simple measure to help you clearly determine your progress in meeting your goal and whether you have achieved it or will achieve it in time, you're done. If not, try more sophisticated measures until you can meet those requirements. A simple measure would be to ask customers how it's going and how satisfied they are. A more sophisticated measure could be a random sampling of surveys received, a mystery shopping telephone interview process, or a statistical analysis of customer ratings correlated to sales.

Accountability

If you have a goal that says you'll generate $20,000 in sales of a given product there's not much confusion about what you're on the hook for. That level of specificity and clarity about what you're accountable for is hard to mask. That's what measures should do. They should clearly tell you if you did or are going to do what you said you were going to do.

Lack of Competence

Picking the right measure is indeed important because if you don't you can get unintended behaviors. When I got my master's degree in teaching, there were no jobs, especially for a teacher with a master's degree who would require a higher salary. My brother, Steve, gave me some good advice. He said, "Corporate training is a new and growing field. Work to just get in the bank (Bank of Boston) as a Teleservicing rep (a vastly growing area), and let them see what they have in your skills." It was good advice. I learned a lot during that time.

One lesson I learned regarded measures. While I was on the phone I sat across from an individual whom I'll call Sara. Each day every representative was measured on average speed of answering calls, number of calls handled, and number of paperwork items handled. Paperwork items were things such as address changes that came through the mail and were done in between phone calls. Each morning our stats would be written on a big whiteboard for each of those three measures. The first week I was there, Sara had the top score on each measure every day. I'm a competitive person, and while I understood I was new, it frustrated me that I wasn't on top. So I started to pay particular attention to how Sara spent her time to learn what she did that made her successful so I could learn from her. It was easy to do because we were in adjacent cubicles that had half walls.

I was shocked at what I discovered. Sara's average answer speeds and volume scores were so high because she often "accidently" hung up on the customers. Or she didn't wait until someone else was on the line to receive a call she was transferring, a company practice. Or she quickly got people off the phone before they could ask another question. Her paperwork score was so high because she literally threw half of the address changes in the trash when she received them each morning, allowing her to get additional paperwork items to handle during the day. Without a measure of quality and completeness, those three measures promoted bad behavior. (I also learned a great deal about ethics that first month.) This was before the bank had the resources to invest in a monitoring system or mystery shopping to determine quality. So although you don't want to overthink measures, you do want to make sure they tell you the story you need them to tell you to drive the right behaviors.

Measures can be as complicated as you want them to be, but more success generally comes with simple measures. Determine measures based on your answers to these questions:

- How will you know early enough that there's a chance you might not be successful so you can do something about it?

- If your stakeholders have said, "Wow, this was really great because …," what happened? What will you see?

- If you don't measure, what's the downside? What's the risk? Is it worth the time (expense) of measuring?

I used to work with toy designers. They tried to tell me that it's really hard to measure innovation. I asked them how they knew that a product had a successful product review. They answered that if their chairman liked it and it made it through the review process, then it was a success. I then asked, "What's in the chairman's head that's telling him that it's a good design? He must have some type of subconscious checklist he's going through, and the prototypes that pass the checklist get a green light. Find out what's on that checklist."

The whole concept of "maybe we shouldn't bother measuring" can be scary for some people. I heard a great story about Wal-Mart that helped clarify this concept for me. Wal-Mart used to take every order it received from manufacturers and check every box against every packing sheet. The amount of money and time they spent doing this was worth far more than what they saved on the rare occasion that an item was found missing from a box. So Sam Walton, the creator of Wal-Mart, made them stop checking every box and instead use a random sample approach. If they determined that they had consistent discrepancies from a specific vendor over time, then they would investigate further. It was more cost effective to significantly reduce the measuring they were doing.

Richard Chang has done some nice work regarding measurement. He's the CEO of Richard Chang Associates and was the Chairman of the Association for Talent Development. He's a master at developing tools and frameworks that make measurement easier. I've used Richard in several companies because he's proficient in so many areas. He's written some good books that are worth reading, particularly *Performance Scorecards*. It takes the concept of the Balanced Scorecard and puts it in a simple, easy-to-understand framework.

One powerful tool he uses is his formula for writing a good goal.

By answering some simple questions (To? What? By? When?), you can write a good goal:

Goal Component	Explanation
To	Use an action word or verb here to start.
What	What's the business result you're trying to get?
By	To what degree do you need to do this? What's the target?
When	When does this need to be done by or how often?

Here are a few examples:

Goal Component	Example 1	Example 2
To	Increase	Produce
What	Employee engagement scores	Ten new designs
By	Ten points on the top three issues	Half of which make it to production
When	By the next survey in six months	In the 2015 product development cycle

This formula is tried and true and works for all size companies, in any industry, throughout the world. And it's simple.

TIP #3

Get buy-in from your customers and suppliers.

Customers

It seems quite obvious that you should be sure that what you're outlining for performance expectations is what your customer wants. But the reality is that most people don't ask. They assume they know. This is a really important piece of the puzzle.

First, I define customers as anyone to whom you hand things off. With this definition, customers can be internal or external. They can be peers or your manager. By being clear on who in your circle receives your "products," you can then ensure you're meeting their expectations.

Asking customers for input:

- Allows you to align expectations.

- Helps align everyone in the organization to achieve larger, overall goals.

- Gives you insights on what to use as measures.

- Is critical to your success. You aren't the judge of your worth, your customers are.

Asking is easy if you know the right questions:

- What are your key priorities this year?

- What would you like to see from me/my group this year?

- What do you need more of and/or less of regarding what you receive from me/my group?

- At the end of the year, if we were your most valuable partners, what has happened to make you say that?

Getting this clarity from your customers can sometimes help you use resources more wisely. I was working with a team that was receiving an 88 percent satisfaction rating on product delivery. The team had operated at this level for some time and had decided to rally to get this satisfaction rating up to the mid-90s. To accomplish this goal, it was going to take some serious effort, some investment, and significant people allocation, so the team decided to do a comprehensive customer satisfaction study. The results of the study were then to be translated into tasks with responsibilities assigned to team members so they would be able to manage the improvement effort using a project plan.

As people began to have conversations with customers about what it would take to bring product delivery satisfaction ratings to the mid-90s, a common question emerged from the customers. Why? While ratings in the mid-90s would be a great target, customers were pleased with the current results the vast majority of the time. During the conversations, the customers identified other areas they would rather see improved. For example, they would like to see products offered in two sizes. The team then determined that the potential return on investment in improving product delivery was far less than the potential return on producing two different sizes of the product. The team adjusted plans and delivered record profitability as a result.

It's good to ask your key customers at the beginning of your journey to help you establish your performance expectations. But once you've created a good working draft of your expectations for the upcoming year, you should check it again with them. Sometimes what you thought you heard isn't actually what was said. So make sure you've clearly understood your customers by sending your list of expectations back to them for validation and buy-in. By looking at the totality of your performance expectations, your customers can better understand the range of activities you'll be committed to in a given performance cycle, not just the ones pertaining to them. Ideally, this final check is done after you've checked in with your suppliers (see next section).

Suppliers

Once you have your set of performance expectations lined up, double check to make sure you can deliver on them. Many times what we need to deliver depends upon others doing their piece. Before you sign on the dotted line for your own deliverables, take them to the people you depend upon and make sure:

1. They are clear about what you're signing up for.

2. They can deliver what you need so you can fulfill your commitments.

This step is often missed in many functional areas. Sales makes commitments about promotional support to the customer without speaking first to marketing. Product design develops something without working with manufacturing to see how long it will take to produce it. HR lays out timelines for deliverables without checking with the business leaders to see if they can meet those timelines. You see it time and time again, yet this lack of communication is easily avoidable.

This isn't a condemnation. Hard-charging and busy people are trying to get work done. Setting performance expectations takes time, and communicating with your customers, then your suppliers, then your customers again to finalize those expectations takes time. But it's time well spent. This small amount of time spent planning and communicating is a much wiser investment in the long run than not delivering what you need to.

TIP #4

Create an upside for achieving goals and a downside for not achieving them.

It's basic human nature to go where efforts are rewarded. The expression "you get what you pay for" is true. Animals are highly trainable using this approach because it's instinctual. People aren't too far off on this same premise. Thus, it makes tremendous sense to align rewards with achieving performance expectations and to create disincentives for not achieving them.

We'll speak about motivation and compensation in later sections, so I won't go into much detail here. However, it's vital to make the connection between the two because incentives are a major piece of the success formula for achieving performance expectations. When you tap into what drives people's behaviors and link that to the desired results, the potential is significant. Incentives are a broad set of things that motivate people. Compensation is one motivator, but others could be a leadership role, verbal recognition, autonomy, time off, etc. Conversely, you could use disincentives to drive behavior. For example, I know of one trainer in the show jumping world who uses the following disincentive: if the riders have time faults, the trainer cuts off a piece of their hair. So the incentive for going fast is that the riders win the class and win money. The disincentive is that, if the riders don't go fast and have time faults, they lose a lock of their hair. Extreme but effective.

Make sure you are incenting the right behaviors. Remember my example of Sara from earlier in this chapter? You can see how measuring speed and volume but not quality encouraged her to behave the way she did. We're often incented directly or disincented in some way regarding performance. That's why having clear measures of what's expected is essential in encouraging the right behaviors to get the results you want.

TIP #5

Work your plan, and if things change, rework it.

What at first looked like a great plan for delivering what your customers needed and expected might not work out exactly as you thought it would. Conditions change and therefore performance expectations often need to change. At least your plan on how to deliver what's needed should change. To be clear, I'm not advocating that a business unit not deliver their numbers. Sometimes conditions change, but in spite of that you may still be on the hook to deliver even though it's become much more difficult to do so.

It's different, of course, when a performance expectation can't be delivered upon at all. For example, if you're to be the project lead of a system implementation and a decision is made to defer the investment for two years, your performance expectation should be changed. (I've been asked what to do during a performance review when a performance expectation that was agreed to at the beginning of the year could not be fulfilled for a reason outside of the person's control. The answer is that the performance review is not the time to be dealing with that issue – it should have been dealt with during the year when the changing dynamics were occurring.)

If you experience a similar situation – when a performance expectation can't be delivered upon because of changing conditions – ask these key questions:

- Is there any part of the performance expectation that can still be executed?

- What should the performance expectation be replaced with?

Don't assume that employees and managers are on the same page about this issue. Employees should be assertive in determining the answers to these questions, and managers should be proactive in thinking about and addressing the issue.

TIP #6

Be public about your work and commitments.

Say you want to lose ten pounds. You think about it only to yourself and tell yourself you're going to lose the weight and quietly modify your behavior to do so. You might be successful if you're very committed to losing it. However, if you were to tell five people you see daily that you're trying to lose ten pounds in the next six weeks, you might have a better chance because they might help you achieve it. They may ask you how you're doing in meeting your goal. If you go for a bowl of chips, you might get a look. If they see you walking five miles, they might say something encouraging about how hard you're working toward your goal. That public commitment raises the stakes on your goal and also helps you because that external accountability – perceived or explicit – creates a little pressure on you to deliver.

The same is true with performance expectations. The more public they are, the more accountable you are and, generally, the more support you'll have to achieve them.

One of the best examples I've seen of this approach was at a factory near St. Petersburg, Russia. As I was walking through the factory, I stopped at a wall that held large sheets of paper with information on them. I asked the factory manager what the information was about. He said it was a list of the goals for each team. Every team had an individual team goal and a shared goal for all of the teams' combined performance. He said that the teams helped each other, pushed each other, and openly discussed performance when a team wasn't delivering because it had a direct impact on their bonuses. He also said that each person was given a rating by their team and the other teams they worked with as to how collaborative they were and how much they contributed to the results. This rating also factored into their bonus. The result was that this factory manager took the performance of that factory through the roof in a short amount of time.

Another example of being public about performance expectations is the process I described earlier in setting them. By querying your customers, checking in with your suppliers, and finalizing the expectations with your customers, you're taking big steps in full disclosure. The trick is to keep being public throughout the whole performance cycle.

TIP #7

Keep it simple.

Marc Effron, in his book *One Page Talent Management,* has the right idea. The simpler, more straightforward we can be in asking for and capturing information, the better. But there are several places this work can be over-engineered:

- The strategic process/cascading takes on a life of its own.
- The measures identified as part of the process become the work rather than the work being the work.
- The forms become the focal point and the destination rather than the vessel of information.
- More time is spent trying to decide what to work on than on doing the work.

The bottom line is that good performance expectations lead to increased individual and business success – managers must commit to setting good performance expectations.

The Chapter's Big Ideas

- Simplicity is key.
- Set performance expectations. It isn't an option to not do this.

- Start with the strategic direction of your business and have performance expectations flow from there.

- Use measures to ensure you get where you want to go.

- Get buy-in from your customers and suppliers.

- Create an upside for achieving goals and a downside for not achieving them.

- Work your plan, and if things change, rework it.

- Strategic intent needs to be cascaded throughout your organization, but so do values and competencies.

- Cascading strategic direction and making it relevant at each level of the organization is every manager's responsibility.

- Fear is prevalent in organizations and permeates activities, leading to diminished results.

- To/What/By/When is a simple formula for setting well-defined goals.

- Look at historical measures and available measures when determining what your measures should be, but make sure you choose the right measures.

- Ask yourself how likely it is that a goal can be met in order to help you decide whether it's worth the time and resources it takes to measure against it.

- Publicizing your commitments raises the stakes and consequently increases the likelihood of success.

SETTING PERFORMANCE EXPECTATIONS ASSESSMENT

On a scale of 1 to 10, with 1 being not at all and 10 being at an industry standard level, rate your organization on the following questions:

	LOW 1 2 3 4 5 6 7 8 HIGH 9 10
1. How well known are your company's values and competencies throughout all levels in the organization?	☐ ☐ ☐ ☐ ☐ ☐ ☐ ☐ ☐ ☐
2. How well can everyone at all levels in the organization speak to the strategic priorities?	☐ ☐ ☐ ☐ ☐ ☐ ☐ ☐ ☐ ☐
3. How competent is your organization at setting good performance expectations?	☐ ☐ ☐ ☐ ☐ ☐ ☐ ☐ ☐ ☐
4. How good are you at localizing strategic priorities for your team or function?	☐ ☐ ☐ ☐ ☐ ☐ ☐ ☐ ☐ ☐
5. How well defined is your process of setting goals for your team or function?	☐ ☐ ☐ ☐ ☐ ☐ ☐ ☐ ☐ ☐
6. How inclusive are you of your team in your process of setting goals for your team or function?	☐ ☐ ☐ ☐ ☐ ☐ ☐ ☐ ☐ ☐
7. How much of an actual verbal or written say do your customers have in your goals every year?	☐ ☐ ☐ ☐ ☐ ☐ ☐ ☐ ☐ ☐
8. How well do you check in with your suppliers to ensure delivery of your goals before you finalize them?	☐ ☐ ☐ ☐ ☐ ☐ ☐ ☐ ☐ ☐
9. How often do you revisit performance expectations and revise them throughout the year?	☐ ☐ ☐ ☐ ☐ ☐ ☐ ☐ ☐ ☐
10. How good are your communication mechanisms to your stakeholders about your performance expectations?	☐ ☐ ☐ ☐ ☐ ☐ ☐ ☐ ☐ ☐

SETTING PERFORMANCE EXPECTATIONS ACTION STEPS

For anything you rated less than 9, what are you going to do about it?

Question #	Actions to Take	Timeframe	People to Involve

CHAPTER FIVE

The "How You Are Doing" Conversation

As you can see by the length of the last chapter, the bulk of your talent management work should be done up front in setting performance expectations. If you've done that well, then the rest should fall into place easily. That's not a guarantee, however, so you need to have a method in place to monitor the work of your employees to positively influence it if needed.

The "How you are doing" conversation is actually several conversations you should have over time. Ideally, the manager prompts these types of conversations as much as the employee does.

One of the best approaches to engaging in talent management conversations I've experienced was used by a CEO I worked with who was running a $20 billion business. He met with each of his direct reports once a month, and they discussed one of three topics, in rotation:

- The first month they discussed business performance.

- The second month they discussed the direct report's individual development plan.

- The third month they discussed the succession plan for the direct report's business and the development plans for his leadership team.

If there was an issue on any of these topics between meetings, the direct report would call, e-mail, or meet with the CEO to address it. Because of this approach, the direct reports knew the CEO was serious about each of these talent management elements. They knew he would come to the meetings prepared, having been briefed on each of the topics by his leadership development partner prior to each meeting. The direct reports also knew what was expected of them, which helped them prepare for the meetings as well. Most importantly, because they all came prepared, the meetings were short and productive. By establishing accountability and checking in periodically, the CEO prompted the direct reports to drive similar behaviors in their own organizations. This approach works very well.

It's a good idea to not go the whole year without a somewhat formal check-in on performance. Many companies use formal mid-year reviews. Some use quarterly reviews because their industry changes rapidly. The bottom line is, do whatever you need to do to ensure your people are delivering on their commitments. You do *not* want to get to the end of the year and *not* make your number or *not* get the expected results, especially if the outcomes could have been different had you known about any problems earlier in the year. It's similar to not tracking your bank account balance and just hoping that you don't bounce a check. Hope is not a great strategy. I know it sounds obvious, but it's tragic to see how often progress isn't monitored, which leads to people not delivering the results that were expected and needed.

Here is a list of the top ten things to keep in mind that will ultimately contribute to the success of your talent management conversations:

1. Make performance check-in conversations about the What *and* the How.

2. Be sure you're present and engaged in these conversations so your point of view is heard, messages are clear, and employees can continue or adjust accordingly.

3. Have a clear idea of what "good" looks like and what results you're looking for.

4. Give your employees ample time to think and respond to questions.

5. Establish management routines to help ensure successful conversations.

6. Be accessible.

7. Seek to understand before you seek to be understood.

8. Teach the art of contingency planning.

9. Keep notes.

10. No surprises.

1. Make performance check-in conversations about the What *and* the How.

Addressing performance expectations that have been set is important, but addressing what employees are working on and how they're getting the work done is essential. Those who don't have these conversations are just plainly not fulfilling their obligations and responsibilities and should be taken out of their managers' role. It's that simple. Managers need to manage. Employees expect it and businesses require it. Use the pre-established performance expectations to guide your discussion. Verify whether the person is on track or what support is needed to help them get on track. Validate that the performance expectations are still reasonable and the best use of this person's time and talent.

Once the "What" conversation leads you to believe that your employee is getting the job done, hold the "How" conversation. As you discuss the deliverables, be sure to listen for the ways in which the work is getting done. Discuss the interpersonal engagement going on and the relationship component of "how" the work is getting done. With most efforts, employees need to balance the time it takes to do the work, what it costs (tangible and intangible), and the quality being achieved. Explore this balance in your conversation and determine if it's appropriate for the outcome desired. This trifecta of elements (time/cost/quality) needs to be managed for every work activity. When pressure is put on one of the elements, it affects the other elements. For example, if something is needed quickly, it will often cost more, and the quality may be affected. If costs are limited, the quality could be affected or the time it takes to accomplish the activity could be longer. Establishing a good balance between these three should lead to optimum results with a better return on investment.

An additional issue to explore in your performance check-in conversations is how your employees are being engaged. Poor communication derails many work efforts. During your conversations, determine whether your employees are having the right levels of communication and engagement with their stakeholders. Here are some questions you can ask:

- If collaboration is needed, is it happening?
- If advocacy and sponsorship are needed, are they being obtained?
- If concepts should be socialized to various parties, is it occurring?
- Does the employee have buy-in to what's happening?
- Are the frequency and mode of communication with the employee appropriate?

When wrapping up these performance check-in conversations, it's a good idea to take notes or have the person follow-up in an e-mail to you as to what was agreed upon or major discussion points. Franklin Covey had a great communication program they bought from Shipley and Co. The program had a terrifically clear and powerful motto: "Deny the reader the opportunity to misunderstand." The big purpose of these conversations is just that – deny the employee the opportunity to misunderstand. Good stuff.

2. Be sure you're present and engaged in these conversations so your point of view is heard, messages are clear, and employees can continue or adjust accordingly.

It's hard to provide a point of view or to guide and coach if you haven't a clue about what people are doing and how it's being received. If you accept that your job is about enabling others, then you need to make it a big part of your job to see what's working and what's not.

Management by walking around is an approach I learned from a consultant who was doing some transformational work with BancBoston Mortgage. The concept originated with the founders of Hewlett Packard. The consultant I learned it from drove change by being on the floor, having conversations, and picking up pieces of information that he could then use as context for when bigger issues were being discussed. He did it well and was unobtrusive about it. He had a style that was a bit humble and made people want to speak with him.

Management by walking around is under-used and underestimated in terms of its effectiveness. Daily interaction with your employees helps you really get to know them, and you can absorb much knowledge just by being in their environment. The rewards are many:

- You're perceived as approachable.
- Your team will trust you more, and you will trust them more.
- It will establish accountability.
- Morale generally improves.
- Productivity is increased, often with spontaneous discussions that can add a great deal of value.

To be effective, this practice takes more than strolling through the office. It's an intentional activity structured so you get to know your team more, get closer to what they're doing, and make yourself available to them. Come across as relaxed – you aren't there to create tension. If you can't relax, stay in your office. As a manager you should let employees carry the bulk of any discussions. You should only be responsible for about 30 percent of the conversation, enabling you to listen and observe better. You're on the hook to be sharp, succinct, and clear. Solicit input as you wander, and make sure you spend time with all employees, not just your favorites! Don't march through the organization freaking people out with your intensity. Freely give positive feedback and answer questions, and look for informal conversations as well.

This approach works well not only for those with a conservative style but also for those with dynamic personalities. An executive I worked with, Dave Woodward, had great success in turning around several businesses because he was highly energetic and fully present when engaging employees. He would make the rounds, remember names, ask about families, repeat key messages, ask how things were going, and use that intelligence to have better conversations with his leadership team. He's one of the best leaders I've known. I've coached many leaders to do this well. It's a fantastic way to keep a pulse on the business. If you don't have a lot of time to engage employees this way, schedule it as a meeting on your calendar, as an employee engagement meeting, and treat it with the same respect you would a meeting with your boss. It doesn't need to take long, merely 10 or 15 minutes, but do it once or twice a week. Showing genuine interest in your team goes a long way toward building relationships and creating followership (the willingness to follow you). You'll see good things happen.

This approach can be done virtually as well when you have team members working in different locations. Dropping an e-mail that simply says, "Checking in to see how you're doing, how's the family, how are you XYZ …" or "How was your weekend?" or "Did the kids enjoy the snow?" goes a long way. This can also be done through texting or over the phone. Doing this consistently will build rapport and let your team members know you are thinking about them and care about them. I've found a random e-mail with just "You good?" in the subject line is often a powerful net for good information. It also opens the door for random insights that might be offered that could help you manage them more effectively in the future. I used to do this as a group/team e-mail by randomly sending something funny. Could be a goat video or a cartoon or a quick story that would get everyone to pile on, and we would have a huge laugh which would lead to more laughs and connectivity. This wasn't done often, a few times a month, but it was lasting in terms of bringing the team together, adding levity to the day, and making work more enjoyable.

3. Have a clear idea of what "good" looks like and what results you're looking for.

While the meandering management-by-walking-around approach helps you pick up tidbits of information, you should be crystal clear about what success looks like for individuals or the team. Ambiguity is not your friend in these situations. I've heard leaders say to their employees something like: "Go get started on something. I'll know it when I see it." Often these employees delivered results that weren't what the leaders wanted, so they had to go back and rework them. For example, suppose a marketing manager was assigned the goal of building more revenue for a particular product line. The manager tells the employee, "Go come up with some ideas and get back to me." The employee might come back with different size options or line extension ideas, while the manager was thinking about raising the price or doing a bundle package. The approach the manager took was wasteful and demoralizing to the employee (whose ideas were dismissed because they weren't what the manager was looking for). Leaders should know what the results should look like before they see them or at least communicate to the employees some clear decision criteria regarding what results would be acceptable.

4. Give your employees ample time to think and respond to questions.

Part of your performance check-in conversations should include teaching employees the art of self-management, so when you're not there, they can do things right or catch things they need to adjust. Ask open-ended questions such as:

- What do you think about …
- How would you …
- What could stand in the way …
- What are you most pleased about …
- Help me understand your thinking …
- What do you hope to accomplish by …
- What led you to …
- How can I help?

These are just some sample questions that can lead to self-reflection and educate you at the same time. They're meant to be provocative but not antagonistic.

Give people ample time and space to think about and respond to these questions (as we mentioned earlier, limit yourself to no more than 30 percent of the conversation). While you may have been thinking about these questions ahead of time, it may be the first time the employees have heard them. The idea of allowing time to think is a lost art in many areas of business. In leading by example with this tip, you can create a dialogue, which is where the sweet spot of employee engagement lies.

5. Establish management routines to help ensure successful conversations.

Management routines are a huge factor in making your conversations successful. These are the specific plans that summarize which stakeholders you will meet with, how often, regarding what, and for how long. Most managers' calendars are repetitive and routine. I would argue that even the non-routine elements have a cadence to them that can be planned for and managed.

Management routines allow for reliable touch points that promote accountability and communication between employee and manager. They are easy to create. I've helped most of the leaders I've worked with create well-though-out, disciplined routines. People gain greater efficiency and have a greater impact as a result.

The next page shows two possible ways to brainstorm about what your meetings should look like. Exhibit 5-1 gets us to think of the major stakeholders you should meet with, lay out the purpose for meeting with them on an-ongoing basis, and then determine how long and how often the meetings should be. Exhibit 5-2 gets us to think in terms of frequency first, adding in the topic and length of time for each meeting.

The point is to think about the key stakeholders you should meet with on a regular basis and make a plan for who, when, and what. Use these formats or another, but organize your thinking, make a plan,

Meet With	Purpose	Length	Frequency
My manager (1)	One-on-one, misc.	1 hour	Monthly
Direct reports (7)	Performance, IDP	30 minutes	Weekly
Key clients (6)	Business performance	90 minutes	Quarterly
Peers (8)	Updates	1 hour	Quarterly
Market visits	Store checks	30 minutes	Every other week

Exhibit 5-1. Major stakeholders to meet with.

Weekly	Every Other Week
• Direct reports, one-on-one for 90 minutes • Financial status reports with CFO	• Market visits • Employee lunches • Staff meetings
Monthly	Quarterly
• One-on-one with my manager • Lunch with new relationship	• Key clients for 90 minutes • Peers, one-on-one for 60 minutes • Business updates with CEO for 60 minutes

Exhibit 5-2. When to meet with major stakeholders.

and then make it happen. If you have an assistant, periodically brainstorm with him or her to be sure you have the right people on your calendar. Make it your assistant's responsibility to put your meetings into your calendar and track them to make sure they actually happen. Audit your calendar periodically to verify your meetings. If you make this process routine and easy, you'll stay appropriately engaged with your stakeholders, including your most valuable stakeholder group, your employees.

6. Be accessible.

In this ever-changing, hugely demanding world of work, managers must be accessible. Given today's technology, there's little reason for managers to be out of touch with their employees for very long. If you're not accessible as a manager, you may be sending an unintended message that your employees or their work are not important.

Some leaders have office hours. Some have predictable arrival and departure times so people can drop in to chat. If you're traveling a great deal, figure out a way to be accessible. My teams have always known that, no matter where in the world I am, they can reach me.

If I saw an employee's name come up on my cell phone, I answered every time I could. If I couldn't, they knew I would get back to them as soon as possible. Why? Because if they were calling, they needed something. Otherwise they would have sent a meeting request. The other way they would get an immediate response is if they sent me an e-mail and in the subject line said something to the effect of "Kim – this needs your immediate attention" or "I need you on this ASAP." It was hard to keep up with the 500-plus e-mails I often received each day in my roles at various corporations. These accessibility strategies ensured I could be involved and monitor and help when needed. The onus was on the employees to raise a flag if they needed help and on me to respond accordingly.

7. Seek to understand before you seek to be understood.

This is good advice all around. Looking to see what's going on before rushing in to comment or judge builds better relationships.

8. Teach the art of contingency planning.

Very rarely does life go according to plan. For the important things, you should have a backup plan. Thinking about the backup plan way ahead of needing it is a smart way to ensure consistency and delivery. In our fast-paced world, where goals are set at best half of the time, contingency plans are rarely made. But employees and leaders who deliver repeatedly and reliably use contingency plans.

Contingency planning isn't difficult. It just takes discipline. Exhibit 5-3 shows some suggested steps to help make it easier.

You may not need to implement any of those contingencies, but thinking about them up front, and not in the heat of the moment when a crisis is burning, allows for a faster and cleaner response. Teaching contingency planning skills builds confidence in the people doing the work since they'll know that if things aren't on target, they have options.

9. Keep notes.

Find a place to keep employee performance or behavioral-related results or feedback as they come along. You should probably have

ACTION STEP	EXAMPLE
1. Determine what could stand in the way of something specific happening or achieving specific outcomes.	We are looking to implement a new system in six months. Possible roadblocks: 1. Lack of skilled people to implement 2. Lack of training on how to use the system once implemented 3. Interferes with existing systems and slows down implementation
2. For each roadblock on the list, determine the likelihood of it happening (use percentages).	1. Lack of skilled people to implement (40%) 2. Lack of training on how to use the system once implemented (10%) 3. Interferes with existing systems and slows down implementation (50%)
3. Determine a threshold you're comfortable with in terms of level of risk (percentage).	30%
4. Determine contingencies for dealing with the roadblocks that have a risk threshold that's greater than what you're comfortable with.	1. Lack of skilled people to implement (40%) • Identify temp agencies that can provide people who have the necessary skills • Identify resource centers that could provide a crash course on how to use the system • Hire people from other companies who have used this system 2. Lack of training on how to use the system once implemented (10%) 3. Interferes with existing systems and slows down implementation (50%) • Do a comprehensive needs analysis to determine possible pitfalls • Use project management software to avoid wasting time and do things simultaneously where possible • Ask other companies who have implemented this system where they've had trouble • Ask your implementation partner to scope issues found with existing systems in use

Exhibit 5-3. Contingency planning steps.

a digital place and a paper place. The employees and the manager should both keep these notes. I had an employee who was outstanding at this. She kept comprehensive notes so when it was time to determine how she was tracking against commitments, she was always right. Now you might think that let me off the hook from having to do the same – nope. She held me accountable for any information that came across my desk in terms of her performance. Good for her. She deserved my full engagement on this. She deserved my full support for her good performance.

10. No surprises.

Most managers don't like surprises. I react calmly if I'm told about an issue early enough, especially if I'm told early enough for us to manage differently. I lose my marbles when something happens that, if I'd known about it earlier, we could have done something about. I'm far from being a micromanager. I don't look to do someone else's job or take power or responsibility away from them. My philosophy is "ask for forgiveness, not permission," and I back my people as part of this philosophy. However, I expect people to use their intelligence and not make the same mistakes twice.

Employees don't want to be surprised either. Alessandro Felici, who headed up a large, global, nutrition business based in Italy, cautions you about surprising employees during your performance rating process: "It's very difficult to assess people below average and motivate them. Requires continuous follow up during the year to avoid the surprise effect."

Dealing with Challenges

Mary Beth Hendrick, a technical documentation manager, puts our discussion about performance conversations into context very well. "Face-to-face communication, plain and simple. The best manager I ever had did not micro-manage me, but she checked in on me on a regular basis. She was interested in what I was working on, how it was going, offering suggestions, and making sure I had everything I needed to ensure I could do my job. I like to say that it's nice when my manager never bothers me – that means he trusts me, right? Trust is great, but it's also frustrating that he doesn't seem to care about my work. It makes me less likely to go the extra mile if it's not going to get noticed. When I had a very interested manager, I would have pretty much done anything she asked me to do." Not having "how you are doing" conversations sends unintended messages.

There's so much value on so many levels to having these conversations. A colleague of mine, Tim O'Connor, who is a managing partner at a firm, described a situation where he was glad he had done this talent management work. "I had a very bright and ambitious employee who was often challenging me. The performance management system enabled me to reinforce his role relative to the other team members and set quantifiable goals to hold him accountable. It also offered me the ability to provide him feedback tied to the performance plan and then, at the end of the year, it aided in having a constructive dialogue. Although there were some points of feedback that were not easy to deliver, the employee felt that there were really no surprises in my feedback and that the evaluation was fair."

If, as a manager, you conduct performance check-ins and find that you aren't getting the level of performance or behavior you expected, ask these questions:

- Do your employees have the skills and knowledge they need to do their jobs?

- Are they being incented or disincented in some way that's standing in the way?

- Do they not trust in themselves? Do they need support? Do they need practice?

- Do they really understand what's expected of them?

- Do they believe in what the company is trying to do?

Richard Chang, the people development thought-leader mentioned previously, offers troubleshooting advice for when you're not getting the performance or behaviors that you expect. He says that the reason for the problem determines how you should go about solving it. He argues that there's a common set of reasons that you aren't getting what you want. The following list reflects his thinking, which I have modified and added to as well:

- Lack of Competence = training
- Lack of Compensation = correcting the incentives
- Lack of Confidence = coaching and practice
- Lack of Clarity = revisiting the purpose, message, communications
- Lack of Commitment = coaching, but if it doesn't look like they'll get on board, remove them

It's hard to know everything about your employees, so look for other sources of input about them. Are there reports or written items you can review? Are there conversations you can have with clients? Peers? Direct reports? Fulfill your responsibility as a manager by periodically documenting your conversations about employees' performance so, in the event of problems, you and the company are covered. You're busy, so don't try to rely on your memory for any of this. Given the volume of information you're managing, it's too easy to forget. Make it a management routine to keep a journal (digital or paper) that includes key ideas that you have, important events that happen throughout your day, an ongoing task list, and an up-to-date meeting calendar.

The Chapter's Big Ideas

- Hold yourself accountable for ensuring your people are delivering on their commitments.
- Make the performance check-in conversations about the What *and* the How.
- Be sure you're present and engaged so your point of view is heard.
- Have a clear idea of what "good" looks like and what results you're looking for.
- Give your employees ample time to think and respond to questions.
- Establish management routines to help ensure successful conversations.

- Be accessible.
- Seek to understand before you seek to be understood.
- Teach the art of contingency planning.
- Keep notes.
- No surprises.
- Deny your employees the opportunity to misunderstand.
- Management by walking around is a great management approach.
- Good management routines are essential for success.

MONITORING PERFORMANCE ASSESSMENT

On a scale of 1 to 10, with 1 being not at all and 10 being at an industry standard level, rate your organization on the following questions:

	LOW 1 2 3 4 5 6 7 8	HIGH 9 10
1. How established is your performance check-in process?	☐ ☐ ☐ ☐ ☐ ☐ ☐ ☐	☐ ☐
2. How much do you discuss the What *and* the How during performance check-ins?"	☐ ☐ ☐ ☐ ☐ ☐ ☐ ☐	☐ ☐
3. How engaged are you in monitoring individual performance?	☐ ☐ ☐ ☐ ☐ ☐ ☐ ☐	☐ ☐
4. How well defined and known are your management routines?	☐ ☐ ☐ ☐ ☐ ☐ ☐ ☐	☐ ☐
5. How often do you manage by walking around?	☐ ☐ ☐ ☐ ☐ ☐ ☐ ☐	☐ ☐
6. How close are you to talking no more than 30 percent of the time in your performance check-in conversations?	☐ ☐ ☐ ☐ ☐ ☐ ☐ ☐	☐ ☐
7. How accessible would your employees say you are?	☐ ☐ ☐ ☐ ☐ ☐ ☐ ☐	☐ ☐
8. How often do you develop contingency plans?	☐ ☐ ☐ ☐ ☐ ☐ ☐ ☐	☐ ☐
9. How proficient are you at capturing information on employee performance and behaviors throughout the year?	☐ ☐ ☐ ☐ ☐ ☐ ☐ ☐	☐ ☐
10. How clear is your expectation on when and how to be engaged with your employees?	☐ ☐ ☐ ☐ ☐ ☐ ☐ ☐	☐ ☐

MONITORING PERFORMANCE ACTION STEPS

For anything you rated less than 9, what are you going to do about it?

Question #	Actions to Take	Timeframe	People to Involve

CHAPTER SIX

The "How You Did" Conversation

THE GOOD NEWS is that if you've done what you should have done according to the last two chapters, doing the talent management work described in this chapter should be a piece of cake. All that hand wringing and angst that you had in prior years concerning performance reviews is a thing of the past. The biggest portion of that work should now be done.

Most people have a flutter in their stomachs or cast their eyes to heaven when they read or hear the words *performance evaluation* or *performance review*. Adults don't like to be judged. Adding in a system that's unclear, arbitrary, or subjective just ramps up their anxiety, discomfort, and downright dislike of this whole evaluation activity.

Mary Zeremenko was an assistant to a well-known chief human resources officer. You can imagine what she's seen! She's got a great perspective and well-thought-out opinions of talent management and development. In past conversations, she expressed her sincere frustration toward managers who are just not doing their jobs. "An employee goes into their review feeling a promotion is on the horizon and is shocked to find that their manager advises them they need further development or they'll be 'managed out.' Shocking, but it happens all the time. The employee is deflated and their confidence is compromised. The manager owns the lack of communication." She's right. It's that simple and completely avoidable.

Given that performance expectations have been clearly set, and performance has been tracked well along the way, the performance review should boil down to one question for your employee: "Did you deliver on the commitments you made?" That's the essence of the review. You could expand the review with additional questions such as "Did you do less?" or "Did you do more?" (that's how performance rating scales have come into existence, where 1 = significantly below performance standards and 5 = significantly above performance standards). But the basic premise is the same – did you do what you said you were doing to do?

To hold a successful annual performance review, you need to make sure the following activities have happened beforehand:

- You've done a good job of setting goals and clarifying expectations at the beginning of the year.

- You've modified these goals and expectations throughout the year to reflect the reality of the work and situation.

- You've provided ongoing feedback and coaching to help the person understand how they're doing and how they could do things better.

- You've presented the above information in verbal and written format so there's no misunderstanding.

- You've made a personal commitment to help this person be successful.

If you've done all of these things, then the annual review is a mere technicality. I firmly believe that if topics in that meeting are a surprise for your employee then you should be fired. I'm not kidding. If people are learning about things for the first time during these meetings, what the heck have you, their manager, been doing during the year? It's incredibly unfair to an employee to save up issues to address in their performance review. The end-of-year meeting should be a formality. I often refer to the annual review as the period at the end of the sentence you've been writing all year. It should be a wrap-up on the year and the beginning of a plan for next year.

Before the Review

Employees should drive their performance reviews. They should start with a self-review – after all, they're the most informed on their performance and on whether they've met their commitments. They and their manager should complement their perspectives with input from key stakeholders. It's smart to tap into the key stakeholders to make sure your calibration of "good" and "expectations" match theirs. As a manager, it's also important that you do this to be able to help your employees understand how they're calibrating.

One executive I worked with, Chris Warmoth, who was running a large portion of a company covering Asia and the Pacific, did a terrific job at this. He would ask each member of his team to identify the people they would like to get input from, discuss the list with each person, and agree to modifications if necessary. He would then have his HR person reach out to everyone on the list, asking how each team member performed. He would then review this input, summarize it, and put it into a letter he would write to each team member. The detailed, thoughtful letter would be several pages long. This gesture was much appreciated by his team. He thought he owed it to them to give them a good source of feedback based on how hard they worked the prior year.

It's more than fine to leverage resources, as demonstrated in the example with Chris, to help you be more effective and efficient in the review process. It's common in organizations for HR folks to help write the reviews at the senior levels. An HR partner can be a good resource for a manager in this process. HR can help gather data – business and behavioral – to help the manager. But the process and content need to be owned by the manager.

I often work with leaders to gather input on how employees are tracking against their performance objectives. I prepare a one-page summary for each employee to which their leader would add his or her own perspective. This summary would serve as a complement to the discussion that was led by the employee and as data sources for the final review. My role was as a facilitator to the leader, but at the end of the day the performance review was his or her responsibility.

In a similar situation, I worked closely with an incredibly busy CFO of a large organization and his team. The timing of his performance reviews coincided with several external-reporting obligations (annual report, analyst day), and he worked 18-hour days for two months straight. Because I had intimate knowledge of the team and worked with the CFO closely, I felt comfortable helping him get started on his reviews. I gathered input and created first drafts for him. He wasn't great starting with a blank page, but he was terrific when there was something written that would jog his thoughts and that he could then add to and modify. Even with the input from stakeholders and my first drafts, he would still spend two to three hours writing each person's review. He just needed a catalyst, and my work acted as such. He probably only used 40 percent of what I gave him, but what he created was far better as a result. I have no issue with people helping executives in this way. The intent of people like this CFO is not to get out of doing something, but to do something better than they might otherwise.

The above situation is far different from one I was involved in early in my career. I had just come back from maternity leave. The person I was now working for was the HR executive for a division that was essentially half of the company. My manager told me to write the performance reviews for the direct reports of a particular executive. Not only was I running the training function at the time and this wasn't my job, but I had not worked with this executive or her direct reports before, and I had no knowledge of their work. I was shocked. I was told to do the reviews anyway because the executive didn't have time.

It was a new reporting relationship for me and I was young. And ignorant. I felt like I had to do it. So I did. I did the best I could and researched the direct reports' responsibilities and business results. I looked at their 360 reports. I casually asked around about them. I crafted the best reviews I could, though I thought the process was woefully negligent. I took comfort being told that the executive would be modifying them. Well, she didn't. She delivered them exactly as I wrote them. I was horrified. And angry. A huge disservice was done to these folks, and I thought I had been used as a pawn. To this day I regret my involvement in that process. It was wrong. And I was wrong to take part in it even though I was following directions.

At the time, I felt my hands were tied. In hindsight, if I could do it over again, I would say no. I wouldn't have been fired, and I could have politely said, "After thinking about this, it wouldn't be fair to these individuals for me to do their performance reviews since I don't even know them. I couldn't do them the justice they deserve. I couldn't possibly replicate the job you could do since you actually know them. I'll be happy to help you with something else." Such a response would have several advantages: (1) I wouldn't compromise my integrity. (2) I wouldn't be party to disrespecting these employees by doing their performance reviews. (3) I would send a message but package it in flattery so I wouldn't come across as insubordinate. (4) I offered to help with something else. If the situation were to occur again and if pushed, I would just say no and take the bullet. At this point, I'm pretty clear that life is too short to compromise yourself for anyone. To help managers develop managerial courage, I often have them play the "What's the Worst That Can Happen" game. Usually the worst possible outcome is not that bad, and doing what you should is worth the cost. Lessons learned and the experience were priceless.

One tool that could have helped the above HR executive keep track of what was going on with her employees is a simple sheet such as the Performance Thought-Jogger on the next page. By taking five minutes to complete it each month, her reviews would be largely written. Summarizing each month's sheet on one document would be short work. A shout out and credit for this simple tool goes to Richard Chang. He's a genius at providing tools. Check out his work – it's activity-based and he gives you great ideas and resources to get your work accomplished.

PERFORMANCE THOUGHT-JOGGER	
Team or Individual Should	
Do More	Continue To
Do Less	Learn About
Start	Assume Responsibility For
Stop	Other
General Description About This Team or Individual's Performance	
Pluses	Minuses

© Richard Chang Associates

Performance Ratings

People can get tripped up with ratings. Keeping things simple can help. What did we ask of our employee? Did they do it? Did they do more? Did they do less? Targets and performance expectations should be robust and challenging to achieve. They should clearly establish what success looks like. If you have a particular performance or behavioral expectation, or a particular person whom you think might split hairs on ratings, you need to take the time to clearly define your ratings – what doing it (meets expectations), doing less (below expectations), or doing more (outstanding) look like – so there's no misunderstanding. Remember the motto from Franklin Covey: "Deny the reader the opportunity to misunderstand." That holds true here as well.

In a matrix organization or in an organization with multiple business units, you need to make sure you have consistency in the way you rate so you don't create issues with employees who compare ratings in different functions, business units, or geographies. Alessandro Felici says a "cross-country or functional distribution rating has to be consistent. The supply chain functions at a previous company were rated and calibrated at the European and the global level. People in the Italian organization had high ratings but were not perceived as top performers by the organization. The whole rating system lost credibility; managers who were perceived to be poor employees got high ratings continuously. Companies have to make choices on functions vs. geographies. You cannot mix the two in a matrix. If you do, you must have dedicated resources to make you vigilant and painfully consistent."

Calibration Sessions

To ensure that fair, consistent, and equitable ratings are given across the organization, many companies hold calibration sessions. These meetings consist of raters discussing employees, their performance, and their ratings and comparing employees to one another to be sure the ratings mean the same for all managers. Because ratings should drive bonus and merit increase decisions, it's important that top performers are identified and agreed upon. Non-performers or low performers should be discussed as well. The reality is that the vast majority of the conversations cover these two groups while less discussion happens concerning employees who are meeting expectations. The point of the meetings is to differentiate top from average performance and low from average performance and to be in agreement on what top, average, and low performance look like. If time permits, it's best to have a robust discussion about all employees.

Rating calibration sessions are held toward the end or at the end of a performance cycle. They are typically organized and run by the HR partner but can be run by a senior leader. All of the key leaders and managers of a particular function or business should attend and be part of the discussion.

The key to a successful calibration session is preparation. Preparation is best if it includes the employee, suppliers, and customers to develop a well-rounded view of the employee's performance. Many companies often ask employees to complete a one-page summary on their performance that can be used as a thought-jogger in the calibration meeting.

These steps should be followed in planning a calibration session:

- HR should organize the meeting.

- Managers should solicit input on their team members and determine ratings for each individual.

- Managers should have discussion notes for each person.

- Managers should submit ratings for each team member to HR prior to the meeting.

- HR should summarize all the ratings from all of the managers. Color coding – attaching a specific color to a particular function or team – can help reveal trends or patterns of ratings more easily.

- HR should create a visual with a summary of the ratings.

During the meeting:

- HR should facilitate the meeting.

- Discussion should begin with employees who are being given above-average ratings.

- Managers should explain and justify why these employees are receiving above-average ratings, and other managers should engage in the dialogue to substantiate or challenge the ratings.

- Once all of the employees with above-average ratings are discussed, those with below-average ratings should be discussed.

- Managers should explain and justify why these employees are receiving below-average ratings, and other managers should engage in the dialogue to substantiate or challenge the ratings. Decisions should be made for how these employees should be managed going forward and put into a performance improvement plan.

- As time permits, discussion should follow concerning key employees who are receiving average ratings or employees whose ratings surprise.

During the meeting, managers should:

- Be very involved in the conversation of both their own employees and those employees on other teams.

- Stick to the facts where possible. Where opinion or perception is used, label it as such.

- Be constructive with feedback. It's for the betterment of the employee and the organization.

- Work to be courageous and honest.

Managers should take notes during these sessions. If they learn new things about their employees during these sessions, they should follow up to get more input. These insights should be shared with the employee either after the calibration session or in the performance review meeting, if that will be occurring soon after the calibration session.

These meetings are extremely helpful for managers to get perspectives on how their employees are being perceived. Managers should come to these sessions with an open mind to fully understand how their team's deliverables compare to those of other teams. These sessions are also helpful in diminishing the roles of politics and favoritism that sometimes play in organizations. By having to substantiate and defend ratings, managers have fewer opportunities to base decisions on relationships (vs. performance).

Some pitfalls to be mindful of during the calibration sessions:

- Not dealing in facts
- Being defensive or reactive
- Letting personalities influence ratings

- Protecting your employees so you're prevented from hearing valuable feedback

- Dealing with things outside of this year's performance cycle – let history stay historical

- Spending too long in one area or on one person or going overboard with the inputs of one person

An important ground rule in calibration sessions is confidentiality. Peers should be able to speak freely to get the best job done in calibration. However, if valuable feedback has been shared regarding an employee, their manager should pursue this feedback in the meeting, if time permits, or after the meeting so they can bring the message back to the employee.

The Form

I wish I had audio that played when you read this. It would sound like a dramatic deep voice followed by music that went dunt dunt dunnnn … People get so crazy about filling out *The Form* during the performance review. Who cares about the form? It's not the important part. The only person who really likes it is the person who created it. If ten people were to sit down and create their own forms, they would be largely similar. But people don't really recognize that and love to fuss about the form and make that the issue. What is important is that you get the message across regarding how well people did against their commitments. If you can't do that well enough with a particular form, add a Word document and expand your message there.

What's important about performance reviews is that the same questions are being asked and answered consistently across the organization and that the answers are documented. What's also important is that the manager and the employee are answering these questions together. Questions should include:

- How well did the employee do what they said they were going to do? (Be specific and relate to each performance expectation.)

- How did they achieve these results? (If there's a company leadership or competency model that outlines expected behavior that everyone understands, use it as a reference.)
- How did they do in developing the competencies they committed to develop in their individual development plans?
- What's expected of them next year and beyond?

It doesn't matter whether the answers are captured on a cocktail napkin or a roll of toilet paper, as long as the conversation takes place and the answers are documented. I do, however, advocate that organizations use one form or shared tool when their managers lead people in multiple businesses or geographies. For example, I've worked with IT leaders who have employees working in multiple continents. With ten performance reviews to complete, they didn't need to waste their time in getting acclimated or in modifying their approach to using ten different forms or tools.

Sometimes there are advantages in using sophisticated tools, such as electronic tools or platforms designed to help move the steps of the review process along. Having reminders of timelines and deliverables due that automatically appear in employees' mailboxes helps busy managers. Having the ability to see who is on track in completing their responsibilities and who isn't can be useful for managers and HR people in determining who needs extra support. Regardless of what tool you use, be sure to capture agreements somewhere. Having a document of some form that captures the performance agreements for a given timeframe, one that's always available to the manager and employee, helps facilitate communication and, at the end of the year, aids in preparing for performance reviews.

I've seen many organizations not set performance expectations well or manage performance well because they were waiting for the perfect form or tool. I was working in a global organization that was scheduled to have an SAP operating system installed; the system was supposed to be the salvation for all things performance management. Five years later there was still no SAP HR module. Valentino D'Antonio, head of HR for an Italian business, took the work into his own hands. For less than $10,000 he had an IT person and an HR person work together to build a homegrown performance management system. It was essentially a workflow tool. It captured input using a five-step process ranging from goal setting to final performance reviews. It pushed the process from start to finish. Once a step was completed, it moved to the next step. It had system-generated reminders for managers on performance management activities. The communications or reminders were based on what work was done or, more importantly, what work wasn't done. Valentino had come from Procter and Gamble (P&G). He knew the value of having tight performance expectations and the impact those expectations had on the business. This Italian business enjoyed a significant turnaround, in large part because of the changes made to their approach to talent management. Technology can help, but don't let it limit you. Don't let it complicate the process. Any piece of paper can be your catalyst. There are no valid excuses for any business to not manage its talent well.

I recently connected with another colleague of mine, Dave De-Filipo, the Chief Learning Officer at BNY Mellon, on this topic. We had worked together at Bank of America previously. I solicited his input on how he thought the performance review process could be made better. He said, "One: Keep it simple (for example, keep the PMP – performance management process – to one page). Two: Don't over-rely on technology – the job of leaders and managers is to use judgment based on facts and observations. Three: Give direct feedback (positives and weaknesses) even if you think it is too much. Employees want to know where they stand." Really well said.

To help make the performance review process straightforward, be sure you have the following:

- The agreed-upon performance expectations that were established at the beginning of the year

- Your performance thought-jogger sheets on the employee

- Feedback on the employee, formal and informal, from others

- Your notes on the employee's performance and behavior – electronic and paper-based

- Business results related to the employee's work

- Project updates or other reports on the employee's work

- Any developmental information – 360, IDP – on the employee

- The employee's self-assessment

- Anything else that can provide good and clear input for how well the employee did to fulfill commitments

Tips on Having the Performance Review Conversation

- I have always liked to conduct performance evaluations during meals. For the most part, employees work incredibly hard, and giving them a break from the day and buying them a nice lunch or dinner is a good way to package the message.

- Always deal directly, succinctly, honestly, and with caring for the person when you deliver a review.

- There should be no surprises in a review. None.

- The review should be a dialogue. Make sure you're creating opportunities for the employee to engage in the discussion.

- If there's an issue that's going to be tricky for you to address, practice with someone. That someone could be HR, someone at home, yourself in the mirror … just make sure the first time you're addressing this tricky issue is not in front of the employee.

Performance Improvement Plans (PIPs)

Sometimes, in spite of all your effort, the performance level delivered by your employee is not what was expected or needed. If the gap between expectation and delivery is significant enough, or if the employee consistently underperforms, you may need to work with HR and the employee to create a performance improvement plan. You want to get the right resources in place to help the employee improve their performance. While you may not normally like to introduce such a degree of formality, it's difficult to go back and put things in place that should have been put in place before – such as HR engagement and documentation. It's a good idea to rehearse the conversation you plan to have with your employee with HR prior to the review meeting to ensure you and HR are on the same page.

Make sure the following is done as part of addressing poor performance:

- Review all prior documentation about performance expectations.

- Check whether you have clearly communicated the performance expectations. If you find you haven't, that's the place to start. Clarify the expectations and carefully document them. Make sure you and your employee review and approve this document. Once this has been done, it's time to create a PIP.

- Review the PIP with your employee in a formal meeting with HR present. Let the employee read the total PIP. Make sure it's written in clear language and includes clear suggestions for improvement. Make sure you include examples of what improvement would look like, focusing on behavior or results. Do not include any judgmental or inflammatory language.

- During the meeting, engage in dialogue with the employee. If he or she can add ideas on how to improve, success is more likely. Listen to the employee's concerns and address them as needed.

- Make sure the employee knows that if their performance is not improved (and that they know to what degree it needs to be improved over what amount of time), they will be terminated. Make sure this is expressed verbally and in the written documentation.

- As their manager, part of your preparation for the meeting should be to anticipate all of the possible reactions your employee might have. Reactions can range from hostility to denial to putting the blame on someone else to appearing to not care to acceptance of the PIP and dialogue about how to improve.

- A PIP should be signed by you and the employee and put in the employee's file.

- Monitoring performance becomes even more critical when a PIP is in place. Tracking the employee's performance and formally documenting discussions you have with them is essential, either to help them get back on track or to lay the foundation for firing them.

Make your life easier by laying the right foundation at the beginning of the year by setting good performance expectations for your employees. And tracking their progress throughout the year will make their performance reviews non-events.

The Chapter's Big Ideas

- If you've done what you should have done according to the last two chapters, doing performance reviews should be quite easy. This is assuming that:

  - You've done a good job of setting goals and clarifying expectations at the beginning of the year

  - You've modified these goals and expectations throughout the year to reflect any changes in the work or the situation

  - You've provided ongoing feedback and coaching to help your employees understand how they're doing and how they might do things better

  - You've presented the above information to your employees in verbal and written format so there's no misunderstanding

  - You've made a personal commitment to help your employees be successful

- The intent of performance reviews is to verify that employees did the things they said they were going to do.

- Self-reviews are important; employees should drive the bulk of the discussion at each performance review meeting.

- Peer reviews are helpful tools for getting a balanced perspective on your employees.

- Solicit input from clients and key stakeholders as part of your review process.

- The thought-jogger, used monthly, can make your performance reviews much easier to prepare for.

- If there are significant surprises in the employee's performance review, their manager should be fired. No joke. They didn't do their job so they should be taken out of role.

- Managers have different opinions on what "good" looks like, so conducting calibration sessions is a smart way to ensure equitable ratings.

- *The Form* doesn't matter. Feel free to document the review on a cocktail napkin (but make sure you do document it).

- If you use technology, keep it simple.

- Sometimes an employee underperforms – when that happens you should create a formal performance improvement plan.

PERFORMANCE REVIEW ASSESSMENT

On a scale of 1 to 10, with 1 being not at all and 10 being at an industry standard level, rate your organization on the following questions:

	LOW 1 2 3 4 5 6 7 8	HIGH 9 10
1. How easy yet effective are your performance reviews for both managers and employees?	☐ ☐ ☐ ☐ ☐ ☐ ☐ ☐	☐ ☐
2. How much do you solicit input from key stakeholders to capture formal feedback?	☐ ☐ ☐ ☐ ☐ ☐ ☐ ☐	☐ ☐
3. How often do you let the employee drive the performance review process?	☐ ☐ ☐ ☐ ☐ ☐ ☐ ☐	☐ ☐
4. How well do you capture and document input and performance results throughout the year?	☐ ☐ ☐ ☐ ☐ ☐ ☐ ☐	☐ ☐
5. How good are your calibration sessions?	☐ ☐ ☐ ☐ ☐ ☐ ☐ ☐	☐ ☐
6. How defendable have your ratings been in the past because you have the right level of documentation?	☐ ☐ ☐ ☐ ☐ ☐ ☐ ☐	☐ ☐
7. How proficient are you at developing performance improvement plans?	☐ ☐ ☐ ☐ ☐ ☐ ☐ ☐	☐ ☐
8. How much do your employees look forward to performance reviews with you?	☐ ☐ ☐ ☐ ☐ ☐ ☐ ☐	☐ ☐
9. How much does technology add to your performance review process?	☐ ☐ ☐ ☐ ☐ ☐ ☐ ☐	☐ ☐
10. How accountable are managers for no surprises in the reviews?	☐ ☐ ☐ ☐ ☐ ☐ ☐ ☐	☐ ☐

PERFORMANCE REVIEW ACTION STEPS

For anything you rated less than 9, what are you going to do about it?

Question #	Actions to Take	Timeframe	People to Involve

101

CHAPTER SEVEN

The "Money" Conversation

You get what you pay for – in whatever currency you want to name. While this section is titled "The 'Money' Conversation," it's meant to convey the idea that you need to use incentives and use them appropriately. It's key to your talent management success. You have many incentives at your disposal. There's a good book by Bob Nelson, *1501 Ways to Reward Employees,* that can help you identify a variety of incentives for employees. You just need to be intentional about what you want, reward the stuffing out of it when you get it, and don't reward it if you don't get it. Sound simple? It should be.

Although I'm not a compensation expert, I can discuss compensation in the context of talent management. If you're looking for a technical discussion of compensation, there are plenty of good books on the market: *Strategic Compensation* by Joe Martocchio is a good place to start.

Lack of Understanding

If you looked at employee engagement surveys from different companies across the world, I bet you'd find, in the majority of them, that how well employees think they are compensated is one of the lowest-rated items on the survey. Most people think they could and should be paid more than they are. While this may be true for some organizations and some jobs, the reality is that most people are being compensated commensurate with the work being performed. But fair compensation isn't the real issue that's revealed by these surveys – *perception* of fair compensation is. As simple as it sounds, communication plays a huge role in clearing up employees' misperceptions about their compensation. Many people don't understand how they're paid, why they're paid the way they are, and what the company thinks about pay. In the absence of this information, employees draw their own conclusions, which generally make the company look bad or make the company look like it has an advantage over them. Communication and understanding go a long way toward demystifying the compensation for employees and managers.

As we read in the first chapter, there are a few fundamentals of compensation everyone should be clear about:

1. People expect to be paid fairly for a job well done.

2. People should be paid fairly compared to other people who do similar work and have similar years of experience.

3. Some places are more expensive to live in than others. Therefore, people need to earn more money in those places to be able to afford taxes, houses, and other expenses that are higher.

4. Companies should decide what they could offer potential workers in exchange for their good work. Is it only money? Is it company reputation? Is it better treatment? Is it opportunities to grow?

5. A company is better off if it has a compensation philosophy. A compensation philosophy puts a stake in the ground as to how competitive the company will be in terms of rewarding its employees. For example, a company may say it wants to be in the 75th percentile of compensation in its industry. What that means is that, out of 100 percent of the people being paid

by companies in that market and in that function and of a similar size, the company commits to paying its employees better than 74 percent of the people. (There are all sorts of compensation studies that can provide companies with this information.) With a distinct compensation philosophy, the company has a defendable and equitable position employees can understand.

6. Compensation issues arise when employees think decisions are arbitrary, when they think they're being taken advantage of, when they think promises aren't being fulfilled, or when there's been poor communication and they're left in the dark.

The more consistent and reliable your approach to compensation is, the more you can use it as strategic leverage in your business. Using compensation and incentives to drive desired performance is extremely underutilized – it's not done well in many organizations nor is it used to its fullest extent.

I worked with a gentleman, Mark Fleming, who was a vice president and general manager of a consumer products company. He's been a senior-level leader at several consumer packaged goods companies. He's a hard worker with terrific values, smart, a good leader, and an extremely high performer. With all that going for him, he still struggles in organizations to fully leverage the compensation system to help him drive superior results. His experience is more typical than not. "Having gone through numerous reorganizations and substantive changes in corporate strategy, I'm surprised how infrequently the financial compensation systems were changed to support/enable the needed behavioral and strategic changes. As a result, I've seen slow and inefficient adoption of the changes. I believe in the old adage 'you get what you pay for.' If you want to make a strategic shift, adjustments to the compensation structure should be included."

A big step forward in making sure you're utilizing compensation to its fullest to drive superior results is a deeper and more robust understanding of the components of compensation. Let's explore these various components and start with the basics – salaries.

Salaries

To determine what a job should pay, a job evaluation should be done. This is particularly true if it's a new job or if the job has changed over time. The compensation personnel in companies do the job evaluations, or you can hire external companies to do them. Job evaluators look at the work being done, the degree of sophistication and complexity of the skill set that's needed to do the job, the scope and scale of responsibilities, the geography in which the work is being done, the level of decision making, the level of risk, the budget being managed, etc. The evaluators then compare the information gathered about the job to information that's already known about similar jobs to get a sense for how close any of those similar jobs is to the job being evaluated. Based on all of those comparisons, plus the company's compensation philosophy, the job evaluators establish a salary range for that job and ultimately a salary for an individual. The salary range is designed to be flexible to account for the experience level of people performing the job.

Employees are usually paid in cash. If the work being done by the employee is worth it, they may be paid in other ways in addition to salary, such as benefits, bonuses, overtime, comp time, profit sharing, retirement funds, executive perks, or stocks.

Benefits

Different companies have different approaches to offering benefits. Benefits are expensive for a company to provide. They're usually equal to one third of the salary of the employee. Let's say an employee has an annual salary of $57,000. Benefits would cost the company another $19,000. Add in the cost of workmen's compensation, social security, etc., and this employee is probably costing the company close to $90,000 a year. Benefits can include medical coverage, dental coverage, tuition reimbursement, adoption assistance, and other similar items.

Bonuses (also called annual incentive plans or something similar)

The more specialized the work the employee does or the higher they are in the organization, the more likely it is that their work directly impacts the success of the company. A bonus is a company's way of saying to the employee, "Okay, hotshot, put your money where your mouth is. If you're as good as you say you are and can get superior results, bet a portion of your pay on getting those results." This type of pay is called variable (or at-risk) pay. People can't count on this pay the way they can a salary. But if they've signed up for variable pay and they deliver on their agreed-upon commitments, then they should receive a bonus in addition to their salary. Often if a company exceeds its forecasted performance and the employee significantly exceeds his or her level of committed performance, bonuses can be larger than what the target bonus was. While this sounds great, keep in mind the highly variable nature of performance and the risks involved. Sometimes the bonuses are based not only on the employee meeting his or her commitments but also on the company meeting its targets. That makes sense because a company can't be paying at-risk pay if it hasn't met its targets or if it can't afford to because others didn't deliver. Sales bonuses work the same way. Salespeople often bet a big portion of their pay on their ability to make the required level of sales in a given timeframe.

Overtime

I've sometimes heard people in the United States get frustrated when they hear that some employees are getting overtime when others aren't. Overtime is only given to those in non-exempt jobs when they exceed a minimum number of hours of work in a week. Jobs are categorized as exempt (salaried) or non-exempt (hourly) by the U.S. government based on the type of work being done. I've often heard people grumble about being non-exempt, but if their jobs were converted to salaried positions, they could be earning less because of the amount of overtime pay they would lose. It's illegal to make a job exempt if the work isn't of a nature to be classified as such. It's illegal to work overtime as a non-exempt employee and not be compensated for it. Employees who work overtime without compensation are not doing the company any favors – this practice can get the company into serious trouble.

Comp Time

Some businesses trade extra hours worked or work done on holidays for comp hours (time off). This means that if someone works six hours on Thanksgiving, and it's not part of their normal schedule, the company will allow them to take an equivalent amount of time off at a later date. Other companies give 1.5 or 2 times the amount of time back to the employee to use as time off. So if the employee worked six hours, they would get nine or twelve hours as time off. This is in lieu of overtime pay. Comp time is practiced mainly in the United States.

Profit Sharing

Some companies have the philosophy that employees should be able to share in the wealth that they've helped create for their organizations. These companies identify a threshold required for profit gains (needed in order to keep the company healthy) and allocate the surplus profit to the employees. The profits are split among employees based on hierarchy or tenure.

Retirement Funds

Often companies make it attractive for employees to save for retirement by establishing a fund in which they can put (typically) pre-tax dollars. Very often companies will match contributions made to accounts such as these up to a certain amount, usually after the employee has been with the company for a certain period of time.

Executive Perks

As a way to attract experienced and talented people to take difficult senior roles, companies often offer additional incentives. These can include life insurance policies, car allowances, special medical packages, club memberships, etc.

Stocks

If members of the senior team are expected to have a significant impact on the long- and short-term success of the company, it's common to offer them a piece of the company (stock) as incentive to do a great job and remain with the company for a long time. Often people in these roles have to sacrifice many things in their lives, which is why companies use incentives such as stock to keep top talent at this level. These jobs are difficult and demanding. The rewards should be commensurate with the job. And when you have a good person, it's wise to tie them to the company in as many ways as possible so they stay to do their good work. Often these stock grants are bestowed over several years. Presumably the better the company does, the more valuable the stock, creating incentive for these senior leaders to do an even better job.

I hope these simple descriptions help you understand the components of compensation and the main ideas behind them. Two additional components of compensation that cause grief for managers are annual incentive plans and merit increases.

Annual Incentive Plans and Merit Increases

Quite simply, after the end of a performance year, the financial folks in the organization will take how much money was made from sales and subtract how much it cost the company to produce the sales and run the company. This difference, a.k.a. profit, is then allocated to various places. Some will go to the people who own shares of the company via dividends, some will go to capital investments in the company for large projects, some will go to purchase other companies, and some will go back to the employees in the form of bonuses, profit sharing, and merit increases.

If the company didn't sell enough or their expenses were too high, there may be less profit than expected or none at all. The leaders have a fiduciary responsibility to pay the company's stockholders first, because they are the owners. In some organizations, employees have come to expect a bonus no matter what. It's a foolish expectation because of the risks involved in running a business.

The bonus pool is an allocation based on a division or team's level of contribution to the company's success. When a business exceeds its commitments oftentimes the pool is large and bonuses are large. In most companies, headquarters will supply each division with the pool of money. It's the responsibility of the leadership of each division to allocate those funds. Leaders should reward superior results accordingly, and they shouldn't allocate funds to those who didn't deliver on their performance expectations. That's a hard decision to make. It's real-life stuff. Some leaders don't demonstrate leadership courage by making the tough choices. Rather, they do what's called a peanut butter spread and divvy the funds evenly, regardless of contribution. When leaders do this, their top performers quickly get the message that their extra efforts and tremendous results don't matter – they're not rewarded for their extra work. It's a bad, bad message to your employees, and it occurs far too often.

Differentiation is incredibly important in retaining your top performers. By rewarding your high performers and not your low performers, the weak players will weed themselves out of your organization. These compensation vehicles (bonuses, stock, etc.) are expensive, so you want to make sure you're getting the biggest bang for your buck by investing appropriately – in the people who have delivered superior results for you.

Sometimes a division will allocate a bonus pool according to set guidelines and, at the last minute, a division head or someone from headquarters will change the bonus amount for specific individuals. Sometimes it's done for a valid reason – a leader may decide to reward a more profitable or more successful division, leaving less in the bonus pool for your division. Sometimes it's done for arbitrary reasons based on personalities and politics. Whatever the reason, when it is done it's extremely difficult for managers to tell their employees that their bonuses will be less than expected – the bonus process will lose its integrity and be particularly hard to defend. Leaders need to resist the urge to reallocate bonuses, especially at the last minute, unless there's a clear business reason or lack of performance that justifies the action.

The timing of these allocations is usually after the performance year has ended and when performance reviews are being conducted. Sometimes you may need multiple conversations depending on the process in your company. You may need to give input prior to the formal process to help your finance department budget. You may need to go back to your manager of managers to adjust the bonus pool based on calibration sessions or senior management input. Determine at each step who needs to know what, and make sure you're communicating against these expectations.

The reviews should be used for bonus decisions. Do not communicate anything about a bonus to employees until you have the final amount and approval from HR or your manager. The reviews should also factor into whether someone gets a raise. As with bonuses, oftentimes companies will allocate pools of money for raises. These raises are referred to as annual raises or merit raises. In the past they were sometimes called cost-of-living increases. They are now, more often than not, raises distributed based on how well employees executed on their performance expectations.

Leadership courage needs to be demonstrated when applying merit increases. Usually the pool is small, and the differences between what employees get will be minimal. Therefore, you need to make that gap as big as it can be. For example, divide your employees into three groups: First, employees who didn't deliver on their performance expectations shouldn't get an increase. Hard, I know, but necessary. Second, employees who met expectations but didn't exceed them significantly may get an increase but it shouldn't be the biggest increase. If your merit increase pool is very small, this group may not get anything as well, in order to enable you to properly reward employees who went above and beyond. The last group, your top performers, should get the biggest increase. It will be the best return on your investment. These decisions and conversations can be difficult. What can help is having a calibration session across groups to determine where the money should go.

Ultimately, what you are trying to answer are the following questions, and the dollars should flow according to the answers:

- Did the employees in these groups deliver comparable results?

- Were there exceptional employees during this timeframe?

- Were there any surprises?

It's common to see performance ratings carry over from years prior. However, every year the rating meter and performance meter should be reset. Every year, a new set of performance expectations should be established. Therefore, every year your employee should get a unique and tailored performance review pertaining to that year's performance. The company, the shareholders, and the employees are due that level of respect.

Two critical success factors for the different compensation vehicles I referred to in this chapter are consistency and fulfillment. Employees are essentially entering into a social contract with companies saying, "I'll trade my work for these compensation items." A company that doesn't follow through on any of these items negatively impacts all the employees long term. Don't change the rules arbitrarily. If you are going to change the rules, pull in some people (preferably line employees) to test your messaging to be sure it communicates what you need it to. Managers often don't get the messaging right – they speak from a skewed perspective (unintentionally and due to ignorance or to their filter, but skewed nonetheless) and the resulting impact on employees is not only frustration about the change but disengagement and negative feelings about management. People won't tolerate it over time. If an emergency requires a rule change (for example, the company can't pay out because it's in financial difficulty), these changes need to be communicated well in advance. Then figure out how to avoid this happening again in the future.

Your compensation approach and components should be designed to drive the desired behaviors and results. Ensure that everyone is educated appropriately to fully maximize this strategic business tool.

The Chapter's Big Ideas

- People expect to be paid fairly and equitably.
- Use differentiation when paying bonuses and merit increases to promote top performance and to drive out the weak performers.

- The company's compensation philosophy – how competitive they will be in terms of compensation – should be applied consistently at all levels of the organization and in all compensation decisions.

- Consistent and reliable pay practices make a big difference in creating followership in employees.

- Compensation appears as an issue in most employee engagement survey results, but lack of understanding and lack of communication seem to be the root causes of the issue.

- Sometimes it takes leadership courage to deal with compensation effectively.

COMPENSATION ASSESSMENT

On a scale of 1 to 10, with 1 being not at all and 10 being at an industry standard level, rate your organization on the following questions:

	LOW 1 2 3 4 5 6 7 8	HIGH 9 10
1. How well do the employees understand the various elements of compensation for the company?	☐ ☐ ☐ ☐ ☐ ☐ ☐ ☐	☐ ☐
2. How accessible are managers or HR to answer questions employees may have regarding compensation?	☐ ☐ ☐ ☐ ☐ ☐ ☐ ☐	☐ ☐
3. How reliable are managers and senior managers in paying out according to commitments?	☐ ☐ ☐ ☐ ☐ ☐ ☐ ☐	☐ ☐
4. How fair do your employees feel your compensation actions are?	☐ ☐ ☐ ☐ ☐ ☐ ☐ ☐	☐ ☐
5. How clear, understandable, and relevant are communications regarding compensation?	☐ ☐ ☐ ☐ ☐ ☐ ☐ ☐	☐ ☐
6. How much does the organization adhere to a true pay-for-performance philosophy where the highest results are rewarded first and most?	☐ ☐ ☐ ☐ ☐ ☐ ☐ ☐	☐ ☐

COMPENSATION ACTION STEPS

For anything you rated less than 9, what are you going to do about it?

Question #	Actions to Take	Timeframe	People to Involve

PART III

Developing Employees

CHAPTER EIGHT

The "How You Need to Grow" Conversation

W E ARE ON to one of my favorite talent management topics – development. It's terribly exciting to watch someone reach a new level, and to be part of it is so rewarding. It's humbling and heady at the same time. There is such pride that accompanies watching someone grow.

So why don't more people commit to developing others? It's counter-intuitive to not grow your assets in an organization. Managers don't spend enough time engaging in this component of talent management for many reasons. The most common reason cited is that they're too busy. I think that's bull. We find time for everything else that we value. So why is it the case that development doesn't get the attention it deserves?

I've probed this issue in a number of organizations with lots of managers. I use a technique called "successive whys" to look for root causes. Here's how my conversation with managers typically goes:

> So you're too busy – Why?
>
> Because you have too much work – Why?

Because much of your day is spent firefighting or doing tasks or in meetings – Why? Because you need to be in a number of places – Why?

Because only you have the skills or experience to do those things – Why?

Because there's too much of a gap between you and your staff – Why?

Because you haven't hired properly or developed people to their potential – Why?

Because you don't have the skills or knowledge to develop others or the courage to use your time to do it.

Okay, now we're getting somewhere.

I've done some work with a top leadership and development director, Jody Vezina, at Waters Corporation. She concurs. "Top managers must be trained/educated on how to develop organizational talent. This is a skill that most managers do not have, therefore it will not be accomplished. Once trained, they seem to be more than willing to take the time to work with their direct reports on IDPs."

When managers don't have the skills, it's not a secret. An administrative assistant in a company where I worked represented the view of many employees when she said, "Many managers look at this valuable process as a burden or a 'check-the-box' exercise. Managers need to be coached on the importance." It was clear to her, as it is to most employees, that every employee deserves feedback and mentoring.

I offer another reason that managers don't spend time on development. Many people who are managers shouldn't be. As mentioned before, sometimes people have landed in the role because they were the best at doing work in their functional area. Consequently, they got noticed and then promoted. It's an absurd proposition because one has nothing to do with the other. Doing functional work well is completely different from leading and managing others well.

I was providing executive coaching as part of an executive development program at Harvard. In reviewing results from the executives' Hogan Executive Assessments and their 360s, I focused on two individuals in particular who had areas of difficulty in their roles as managers. During individual discussions with these two managers they disclosed the same facts about themselves: they liked to work by themselves, they liked to accomplish tasks individually, they really didn't like people, and they didn't like being managers. So, what are the odds that these managers will create followership? What are the odds that these managers will create breakthrough growth for a company by inspiring the people under their responsibility? The odds are pretty low. These two managers were in their roles because it was expected of them. They were miserable, and from the looks of their 360s so were their employees. This is the craziness we need to have the courage to change in organizations. So much wasted productivity and frustration occurs at all levels because people are in roles they should not be in.

In one company I worked with, there was a mergers and acquisitions (M&A) guy who was fantastic at M&A. He had strong relationships with banks and was instrumental in getting several deals done. But he was a terrible manager. He didn't like doing it, and he wasn't good at it. His employees hated working for him. This happens often, and when it does the companies wind up with people in management roles who are tortured because they simply don't want to manage.

To be a great manager, you need to care about people. To lead, you need to be committed to them. This is never truer than in developing others. Developing others takes time and commitment. Valentino D'Antonio put it well. "To develop a person you need personal commitment. It is like growing a son or daughter. You cannot delegate it to other people and think it absolves you of responsibility completely. It is the only way to successfully develop a person."

Gregory Wagner of ValueEngager agrees. "In order to be an effective developer of people, one must care about the people and enjoy seeing a positive result from your contributions to their future. If the task is viewed as a required task of a manager ... it is usually done halfheartedly or not at all."

People who get it, people who truly understand and see the value of investing in others and developing them strongly, believe this. Alessandro Felici figured it out as part of his leadership journey. "It's by far the best use of your time. You will never deliver a project with higher return than successful people development. But be ready to do a very heavy lifting job. People development requires maximum effort and time. This is what it takes and all you need to develop a formidable business."

Many employees simply don't reach their potential because leaders haven't spent enough time with them to develop them. It happens at all levels in all geographies in all types of companies. Imagine the amount of untapped potential out there as a result. When people are surrounded by politics, organizational hierarchy, history, etc., developing people is even more difficult.

In one global company I worked for, the Latin American business was struggling. The leader was brilliant and had a sense for product like no one else. The command he had for the numbers was scary. But the problem was, *he* was also scary. Even HR didn't want to work with him. He was volatile and unpredictable. The behaviors he demonstrated created issues of trust in the organization. He spent little time communicating because he didn't feel it was his responsibility to clarify issues – employees should ask questions if they don't understand something. Have you ever tried to ask questions of a volcano? It doesn't inspire confidence, and this lack of engagement trickled throughout the organization. The problem was, he had never been taught how to act differently, and since his brilliance netted good results, his bad behaviors were tolerated and perpetuated.

Now, this leader couldn't be more passionate about the business or work any harder. He and I connected at a leadership program. I said to him, "I think you've been done a disservice. I think you have no idea how you impact people, and if you knew how to act differently, I think you would. When you want to get better results from your employees, come see me." The look on his face was priceless. He was sitting in the chair in my office the following Monday morning. We attached at the hip. He learned quickly and became open to coaching. After 18 months, the Latin American business was one of the most profitable businesses in the company and employee engagement had changed considerably.

I find this is the case more often than not. People who are difficult or angry are often that way for a specific reason. These folks often need the most help but don't get it because they put people off. That's where managers need to do their best work and break through this wall and reach the potential great leader inside that person. Leadership development is hand-to-hand combat in my book. It is eyeball-to-eyeball work. Change happens one person at a time.

The bottom line is that development isn't just a nice-to-do. It's a strategic business imperative and required for ongoing competitiveness. Susanne van Iersel, a supply chain executive, clearly understands the importance of development. "My advice: talent development and top performance of a team or company go hand in hand. You cannot do one without the other. You have to manage both the performance/results and people side of things. If you only focus on performance, you will not unleash the full potential of your team and talents. Your focus will be myopic and short term. Conversely, if you only focus on people and are too soft on performance, you will lose on results to show the added value of the talents. Talents require an investment, but done well, it will pay off in performance! So the trick is to keep working both components ongoing."

Many top companies believe in creating development plans. Kevin Wilde, an accomplished professional who is the chief learning officer at General Mills, says that at General Mills they "use IDPs for *all* professional employees annually to set growth initiatives for each employee with his or her manager."

As a manager, insist on development activities for all of your employees. They should all be working on improving. Think of their skill set, knowledge bank, and experience as a 401k or investment account. They would be frustrated if their balance was the same this year as it was last year. They would not be happy that the equity in that account hadn't grown. So what can and should you do to grow the equity in your employees? The good news is that most employees want development. Lack of development is often one of the top three reasons cited as to why people leave companies. Most people want to do more and be more but don't have a clear path or the right support. Providing that clear path and offering the right support is the most vital part of being a manager.

When I speak with employees around the world, a common theme I hear is "I could do more." People often feel they have untapped potential that's being wasted. "Doing more" sometimes equates to the actual volume of work being done. Often I've visited companies where the receptionist is reading a book in between answering calls and greeting and managing arrivals. She's not wrong in doing this, but what a missed opportunity for the company. I've operated with a lean budget in all of the companies I've worked for. My staff has been limited as well. I often come across people who say to me, "I'm really interested in what your team does and would like to help out if I could. I sometimes have time on my hands so keep me in mind." I applaud people with that attitude, and I fully utilize them. You never know what gems you might find in working with people in this way. I've often tapped into people's detail orientation by having them edit and proof documents. I've helped people develop instructional design skills by investing in them and, in turn, working with them on a project. I've utilized people's research skills in major data-gathering efforts during the needs analysis phase of work.

In regard to your own team, I would bet you five dollars that if I asked everyone on your team today whether they could do more than they're doing today, most of them would say yes. The people who say no are most likely people new to their roles or people who have a huge volume of work and can't imagine spending more time doing work. How am I so confident in my bet? People are underutilized around the world. People want to be more intellectually challenged. Most people want new and different things to work on, particularly with the right guidance and coaching. As a manager, look for people inside and outside your organization who want to do more and want to grow. Invest your time with these people and it will pay off tremendously.

Deciding What to Work On

There are two schools of thought regarding what to work on in terms of development. One school of thought is to have employees focus on the areas in which they aren't proficient or areas that are considered weaknesses. (But keep in mind that the word *weakness* is taboo. I'm not sure why. More candor and authenticity might help dimish weaknesses faster in my opinion.) The other school of thought is to focus on strengths and take them to a new level.

I suggest doing both. If something is standing in the way of an employee's effectiveness because he or she isn't good at it or is actually bad at it, the employee should work on improving it. Additionally, if there's something that someone is good at, they can have a better competitive advantage by taking it to an even higher level of competence.

Carla Diogo, a senior-level person at a well-known consulting company, will tell you to concentrate your efforts on developing strengths. "Strength-based development tools are valuable because they focus on maximizing strengths and navigating weakness vs. developing your weaknesses. Uncover and leverage the strengths to get the most out of your people."

Roel van Neerbos was president of Continental Europe and head of Global Ketchup when I worked at Heinz. He used a tennis analogy that resonated with many people – focus on your forehand. He got a great deal of traction in his organization with the notion that you should maximize your strengths while addressing areas of weakness if they are standing in your way.

The good news is that there are many sources of input to help you decide what to focus development efforts on:

- Performance results
- Performance reviews

- Client or customer surveys

- Feedback

- 360 reports

- Assessments

Let's take a look at what each one can offer.

Performance Results

Are there gaps in performance? Are there new market opportunities that weren't pursued because the capability didn't exist? Looking at trends in performance results may highlight some skills or knowledge areas that are deficient, or areas that are strong and can be applied elsewhere.

Performance Reviews

Considering the results of past performance reviews is a great strategy as part of validating what skills or knowledge areas should be developed in the next performance cycle.

Client or Customer Surveys

Clients are usually good at indicating what they prefer and what doesn't work for them. Surveys may highlight elements that can serve as content for individual development plans.

Feedback

Perspective from others on what's working and what needs adjusting is sometimes the most powerful input for development. An HR director I worked with believes wholeheartedly in using feedback. "There are so many resources out there on this topic and I have leveraged many of them to try different approaches. However, I believe it comes down to basic fundamentals, one of those being candor. People can truly only develop and grow if they are getting feedback, and that feedback has to be direct, sincere, and honest. When people understand how they are performing and where their blind spots are, they can make the choice for themselves. Top talent will always make the choice to improve and change if necessary; that is true development."

360 Reports

This comprehensive solicitation of input from multiple stakeholders is a great way to determine what areas someone is strong at and could take to a new level and what areas stand in the way of their being successful. The term 360 comes from the idea of gathering multipoint perspectives (think about turning in a full circle – 360 degrees) by getting insight from the individual, their manager, direct reports, peers, and clients.

When you get a 360 report for someone you're managing, here's how you should use it:

- Go to the back of the 360 and read the verbatim comments first. This gives you a flavor of what people are trying to tell you in their ratings.

- Next go to the highest- and lowest-rated items and look for trends.

- From there go to the overview section to compare your insights thus far to what the 360 results look like at a macro level.

- Go to the item or question/statement section last. There look to see how spread out the ratings are. If they're widely spread, that indicates that the stakeholders are having different experiences with the employee. Also look to see if there are outliers (which may point out a special relationship between the rater and the employee, either good or bad).

- Look to see how the manager's ratings compare to the other ratings.

- Look to see how the employee's self-ratings compare to the other ratings. A consistently low or inflated self-rating is indicative of a self-perception or communication issue.

The 360 tells you where to spend additional time in gathering information about the employee, either by having more conversations or by doing further research. The results of the 360 can clarify strengths and weaknesses, which will help determine areas for development.

Assessments

Assessments (often psychometric tests) are effective tools for helping you become more informed about people's traits, preferences, cognitive levels, and functional depth. Typically assessments are used to help in employee selection, training and development, career planning, and team building and development efforts. The proper use of assessments can be tricky. Assessments need to be reliable, statistically valid, and representative of the population with which you're working.

If you're going to use assessments, whether you work with an HR partner or not, become informed about the purpose, application, and interpretation of whatever assessment instrument you select. Make sure the assessment process is rigorously managed. Prior to collecting the assessment data, determine who will see the data, communicate that fact, and stick to it to maintain the integrity of the process.

Sometimes multiple assessments are used. Use no more than two assessment instruments at a time otherwise the process can become confusing. I'm an advocate of coupling a behavioral 360 instrument with a personality assessment. I think an inside-out perspective (personality assessment) combined with an outside-in perspective (360) gives great insight into why we behave the way we do and how people see our behavior.

There are many assessment instruments on the market. They can be found in areas such as career profiling (Shein's Career Anchors or the Career Interest Profiler), personality profiling (MBTI, DiSC, Firo B, Social Styles, HBDI, The Power of Understanding People Assessment), and cognitive skill determination (Wonderlic Cognitive Assessment). You can find assessments for specific areas such as emotional intelligence, team membership, conflict management, diversity, etc. There are also a number of assessments that measure functional excellence (sales, finance, HR, administration, etc.). There are some assessments that combine several of these areas such as the Hogan Executive Assessment, a tool I use often. Using the data from assessments provides insight on behavioral tendencies, which makes it easier to be aware of these tendencies and to plan for developing alternative behaviors. If you're planning to use assessments, be sure to research your options so you can make the best-informed decision.

If you're working globally, be sure the instrument you use translates language-wise or concept-wise. On a trip to Mumbai, I was asked to do some assessments with a company's leadership team in addition to having a number of one-to-ones with their top talent. While I knew that the DiSC instrument that they wanted to employ had been used in that country by others working with teams, I tested it for myself by having a friend of mine from Mumbai, who's a corporate lawyer, complete it. (I've used DiSC instruments for nearly 20 years.) Afterward we reviewed the experience and looked for potential cultural or language issues. This first-hand knowledge of the assessment instrument was essential to ensure the integrity of the assessments.

Once your employee has considered potential areas for development, have them reflect on these questions:

- Is there any area that, if you didn't address it, would stand in the way of your achieving your performance goals for next year?

- What development opportunities are there to help you improve the performance of your business?

- Is there anything you can work on that will help advance your long-term goals?

- What is your passion? What do you find energy to work on?

When your employee has selected an area to focus on, he or she should validate the selection with you. You don't want to create a development plan and begin executing it if you think the employee has a burning desire to address another area.

Development takes time and lots of energy. Be reasonable about how much an employee can accomplish in a given time frame. Many development plans have several areas for growth, which can be counterproductive in the long run. Have your employee concentrate on one to three areas to develop.

Next, help your employee think about how he or she will develop. There are many ways to do it. Here are some ideas:

- **Books and articles:** There are many terrific resources available to you, some in digital form so you can use them for quick reference. Subscribing to business magazines such as *Harvard Business Review* or googling topics are great ways to gain information. I've found that one of the biggest predictors of business success is having good reading skills. Reading allows you to refresh and renew your knowledge quickly without much effort. The reality is that most people stop reading when they enter the workforce. A common trait of top performers, however, is that they read often and stay current.

- **Project work:** A great way to improve in an area is to assume some work responsibility in that area, perhaps by working on a relevant project. By sharing the burden of executing a project with other people, you can deliver and develop at the same time.

- **Temporary assignments:** Doing work in short intervals develops skills and knowledge areas in a robust way. In one global company, we used temporary assignments, or secondments, as ways to give employees access to new and challenging areas. Secondments were usually one to six months in duration. They were often international assignments. Afterward the employees went back to their regular jobs, in the same or sometimes a different role. When people tell me that their business can't afford to offer temporary assignments, or that an employee is too important for the business to be without, I tell them to treat the situation like a maternity leave. If the employee were going out on leave, the department or division would need to figure out coverage. They need to do the same here. Often the gap left by the employee vacating their job creates room for others to step up and develop as well.

- **Online learning:** Many companies have purchased classes that can be taken online. Additionally, there are many cost-effective ways to engage in training over the Internet. This type of training is easily accessible and the training modules are often available afterward for reference. As an aside, online learning is a fantastic way to reach many smaller markets or emerging markets. To be able to offer a large number of courses in multiple languages is incredibly desirable for those markets and cost effective.

- **Degree or certification:** If the area of knowledge or skill to be developed is significant and sizeable, the employee might want to think about pursuing a formal degree or certification to establish a high level of competence in that area.

- **Volunteering:** Volunteering serves two purposes: The employees get to contribute to the community while improving their knowledge or skill in an area.

- **Keeping a journal:** Reflecting on what happened, what triggered it, what worked, and ways to do things differently is a great way to develop thought processes or to perfect skills. Setting the journal aside and re-reading it later can greatly increase clarity.

- **Training:** There are many valuable training options available to you, internal and external, formal and informal. Be careful, though – training isn't a wonder drug even though it's often treated as a cure-all.

Jacques Pradels, whom I referenced earlier, is a senior-level executive who firmly believes in continuous self-improvement. Jacques commented on the potential pitfalls of training: "I have had some bad experience around training. Training is a strong tool to increase people capacities, capabilities, and behavior. But some companies aren't consistent in their training practices (preparation, follow up, aligning the company vision and values with individual needs). This inconsistency can lead to frustration, which is the opposite of what we are looking for."

There's a fantastic book called *Successful Manager's Handbook* written by Susan H. Gebelein and others, and published by Personnel Decisions International, that all managers should own (there's a version for executives as well). I've probably given over a thousand of these books away in my roles as chief talent officer to managers around the world. It's not a book to read front-to-back but a book to refer to when you want information about a topic. It's a gold mine for two reasons. The first is that it offers great ideas on developing a variety of competencies. The second is that it helps you and your employees narrow the focus on an area of development. Very often your employees will come to you with overly broad areas they say they want to develop. They might say to you, "I need to work on communication." Well, that's like saying they want to work on world peace. Here's how your conversation might go after that:

> *You:* What specifically regarding communication do you want to get better at?
>
> *Your employee:* I'm not good at presentations.
>
> *You:* What part of presenting is more challenging for you than others?
>
> *Your employee:* I'm pretty good at getting the information out. It's when people start asking questions, especially at the end of the presentation when I don't have a script, that I fail.
>
> *You:* Okay, is there any other area you're not succeeding at in making presentations?
>
> *Your employee:* No, I actually get a lot of good feedback on the rest of the presentation and great feedback on those presentations where there's no question and answer period.

You: So it isn't communication skills that you need to work on but rather you'd like to get more comfortable and competent at managing Q&A as part of your presentations?

Your employee: Yes.

If you aren't skilled at helping your employees narrow the focus on developing specific behaviors or knowledge areas, they can fail quickly. Here's another example of narrowing focus:

Broad Category	Range of Skills	More Specific Skills
Administrative skills	• Working efficiently → → →	• Managing your time • Expediting paperwork • Managing meetings
	• Establishing plans	...
	• Managing staff	...
	• Development systems and processes	...
	• Managing execution	...

If you or your employee can't determine the right level of focus, or find the right words to describe a development area, *Successful Manager's Handbook* can be a great resource.

The best set-up for development is actually a combination of efforts. Two professionals in the early 1960s laid out a learning and development model: 70-20-10. Research by Michael Lombardo and Robert Eichinger showed that professionals learn best when about 70 percent of the effort and input comes from working in challenging jobs or on-the-job learning, 20 percent comes from relationships with people (with the majority of that coming from their boss), and 10 percent comes from courses or reading. So a combination of learning interventions is best and should consist of ones that the manager can support, the organization can afford, and the employee is likely to succeed with.

Not one of these avenues of development can work by itself, and each requires follow-up and consistent attention. Take training, for example. You can attend a great training session, but unless you do specific things to transfer the knowledge beyond the classroom, most likely it won't stick. This is the reason that a number of executives don't invest in training – they think they won't get a good return. If training is done in isolation, you may enjoy a little more employee loyalty, but that's it. If you're involved and the training is reinforced, you'll see a better return.

The best scenario is to develop your employees a little bit, over time, in non-threatening ways. Have them practice. Build in specific work time for practice, feedback, and more practice. Make sure the development activities are focused. And, as with their performance plans, employee development plans should be specific and public and include measures of development.

Employees Need to Commit to Development

Sometimes I come across managers who have decided what an employee needs to do in terms of development. While it's terrific to have a deep level of engagement from the manager in regard to an employee's development, we all know that if someone doesn't want to do something, it's hard to get him or her to do it. An employee has to be engaged in his or her own development. A manager can provide input on what to develop and help employees understand why working on a particular area is beneficial to them, but if the employees don't have passion and commitment then nothing will change.

I was coaching a very senior financial services executive in a company that had a red, yellow, and green approach to categorizing 360 results. If ratings fell below a certain percentile, the results were classified as a possible issue (yellow) or very concerning (red). This guy had a lot of people working for him, was in charge of a significant amount of money, and had 360 results that were all red for the second year in a row. The CEO said that these results needed to change or the executive's job was in jeopardy. I was chosen to work with him.

As a way of understanding the quantitative 360 results, we identified key stakeholders, and I conducted hour-long interviews with each stakeholder. The questions I asked were:

- What are this person's strengths?

- What are this person's developmental areas?

- What should this person start, stop, or continue to do to be more effective?

- If you were this person's manager, what advice would you give him so he can be more successful?

- What would you personally and specifically like from this individual?

- Do you know of anything being said about this person that people may not have the courage to tell him directly?

While this describes the process I used for this individual, it's actually a process that I've used in many organizations. For the 360 reports, the data collected in the interviews is not edited. It's summarized as verbatim comments. The only comments that are attributed to specific stakeholders are ones about what the stakeholder would like personally and specifically from the individual. (The stakeholders are warned that the answer to this question will be attributed to them.) The data is organized around major themes that emerge. The report is often 30 pages long (length depends on the number of stakeholders interviewed). It's a fantastic way to get a comprehensive picture of an employee.

When I use this process now I often couple it with the Hogan Executive Assessment to get a comprehensive inside-out/outside-in view of an individual. It's a powerful way to profile an individual, and I've used it successfully in a number of companies around the world.

Once I created the report on this financial services executive, I reviewed it with him. My strategy is to always review these reports with the person assessed so I can manage the message. Typically this approach has worked well, but it didn't with this executive. When he saw the report, he completely flipped out. It took me five, two-hour meetings to go over the data. At different times he told me that I was irresponsible for actually putting these comments on paper, that I had no idea what I was doing, that he made a ton of money for the company, etc. We held these meetings on the phone and in person. I remember one Friday afternoon phone call. I was in Boston, and he was in New York. He was furious. He asked, "At what point are you going to be questioned on your poor judgment in putting these comments in the report." I said, "It doesn't matter whether I asked the questions or not, people hold these opinions of you. By knowing, you have a choice. I don't edit the data. You see exactly what people think of you. I don't make decisions about what you should hear or not hear of what people said about you because once I do that, you should no longer trust me. I don't care what you do. I don't have any agenda other than helping you if you're ready to step up and take responsibility for your behaviors and work on adjusting them. It's all on you." He hung up on me.

He called me the following Monday morning. He said, "Okay. I've asked around and you apparently know what you're doing. I guess there's a science to this stuff. I'll try it for one year. But at the end of the year I want to be the first guy to go from an all red to an all green 360, and if I don't, I'll have your job." I told him, "If you do exactly what I say and do it with sincere authenticity and you don't get an all green 360 next time, you can have my job." What a year. The guy was a maniac, but bless him, he did exactly what I said and the transformation in his team and organization was remarkable. His results were so significant that he received a huge promotion. None of this would have happened if he hadn't internalized the message and owned the feedback and development.

That's why I'm a fan of employees owning their development plans. I encourage people who work for and with me to identify what they think are key areas to consider for their development, and we discuss those. Granted, the development area needs to be within reason and within the context of the business. I'm not going to support them learning Chinese if we don't have business or partners in China.

I will provide advice but it has to be the employee's choice whether to take it. They need to have some skin and sweat in the development game. They need to feel that it's theirs. Often employees don't have a good source of ideas for this process, and brainstorming with them is very helpful. But it's got to be their gig.

Doing this work on an ongoing basis can help you make tough decisions. While we're talking about doing this work annually and working it throughout the year, new leaders should do it as quickly as they can when they come into a new group or organization. New leaders are often hesitant to make changes in the talent. Here is the issue with that. I've often heard leaders say, "I wish I'd moved on that person sooner." I've never heard a leader say, "I wish I'd waited longer to deal with that person who wasn't capable of doing the job." Not making changes soon enough has often led to the demise of new leaders.

In one company we moved a successful leader from one part of the business to a key area of the company. He had lots of coaching and advice on making the team his own and addressing mediocre performers. While he nodded his head indicating he knew about the mediocre performers, he actually didn't do anything about them. Ultimately the business ended up failing, and he was fired. It was a shame because he had been very successful in other roles, but he refused to demonstrate the required leadership courage that was needed in his new role. The development and evolution of his team was his biggest opportunity and he simply didn't go after it. Understanding where people are in regard to their talent level and development is essential. But being capable of making the tough call as to whether someone is the right fit is where many leaders need to improve.

The Chapter's Big Ideas

- Managers need to care and be engaged for development to work.
- Development isn't a nice-to-do, it's a strategic business imperative.
- Many employees think they have the capability and capacity to do more.

- There are many inputs to the decision on what areas of development to work on, including performance results, performance reviews, client or customer surveys, feedback, 360 reports, and assessments.

- There's a tremendous range of assessment instruments on the market to give you insights on employees.

- There are many aids to employee development, including books and articles, project work, temporary assignments, online learning, degrees or certifications, volunteering, keeping a journal, or training.

- The best set-up for development is a combination of learning interventions, and ideally 70 percent comes from on-the-job learning, 20 percent comes from learning from people, and 10 percent comes from training.

- Development needs to be employee-led and manager-supported.

DEVELOPMENT ASSESSMENT

On a scale of 1 to 10, with 1 being not at all and 10 being at an industry standard level, rate your organization on the following questions:

LOW   HIGH

	1	2	3	4	5	6	7	8	9	10
1. How linked is the concept of development to the strategic intent of the business?	☐	☐	☐	☐	☐	☐	☐	☐	☐	☐
2. How accountable and engaged are managers in employee development?	☐	☐	☐	☐	☐	☐	☐	☐	☐	☐
3. How widely used is a 360 in your organization?	☐	☐	☐	☐	☐	☐	☐	☐	☐	☐
4. How widely used is training as a development solution in your organization?	☐	☐	☐	☐	☐	☐	☐	☐	☐	☐
5. How often do leaders show courage by removing an employee out of a manager role if they're more suited for a functional role.	☐	☐	☐	☐	☐	☐	☐	☐	☐	☐
6. How often do you solicit multiple inputs for someone on your team in regard to what they should work on?	☐	☐	☐	☐	☐	☐	☐	☐	☐	☐
7. Does your organization display breadth and depth in its choices of assessment instruments?	☐	☐	☐	☐	☐	☐	☐	☐	☐	☐
8. How often do you consult resources such as *Harvard Business Review* or the *Successful Manager's Handbook?*	☐	☐	☐	☐	☐	☐	☐	☐	☐	☐
9. How much do your employees (vs. their managers) drive the development process?	☐	☐	☐	☐	☐	☐	☐	☐	☐	☐
10. How much do managers actually care about the development of their team members?	☐	☐	☐	☐	☐	☐	☐	☐	☐	☐

DEVELOPMENT ACTION STEPS

For anything you rated less than 9, what are you going to do about it?

Question #	Actions to Take	Timeframe	People to Involve

CHAPTER NINE

Succession Planning

L ONG-TERM CAREER DEVELOPMENT takes consideration and effort that's different from that needed for simple individual development. Career development needs to be more strategic in nature. Individuals think about careers, but do organizations? Yes, they do (although they approach the subject differently and call it succession planning). Career development and succession planning take into consideration both the individual's profile and interests and the direction of the organization. They're two sides of the same coin. Which one you're primarily concerned with depends on whether you're the individual (career planning) or the organization (succession planning). We'll examine both in-depth.

We'll start by demystifying the succession planning process, which requires a great deal of organizational time and energy, is often done behind closed doors, and about which nothing is communicated after the fact. The absurd element in succession planning is that it creates major distress for the organization that's unnecessary. Transparency goes a long way in this work.

Succession planning starts with looking at the organization's strategic direction and answering the question, "What capabilities do we need in

139

order to execute our strategic plan?" Unless you're ahead of the curve in determining where the organization is going, you won't have the talent levels you'll need to execute your plan. For example, I worked with a brilliant guy at Bank of America, Andrew Odze, who was able to predict, based on the growth of a business, how many leaders would be needed at what levels over what amount of time if the growth was maintained. It served as a call to action for developmental efforts.

At Bank of America they did succession and talent planning really well. The work was executed at multiple levels with many inputs over time. The due date for this planning was always August because that's when the heads of the businesses would meet with the CEO to review plans and make decisions. The decisions were announced a few weeks later, informing employees of any significant changes that would be made to the organization's leadership and structure. It was like nothing I've ever seen. But they really believed that this was a good way to grow leaders and to continue to reinvent the bank.

This is the right path for succession planning. Start with the strategic direction of the company followed by answering the question, "Who in our talent pool can help us execute against this strategy?" Bill Johnson, a very successful former CEO of a large global organization, used to say that the moves have to be good for the organization and for the person involved for it to work. Bill was really good at succession planning, thinking through, long term, how he could invest in people while concurrently growing the business. What made Bill good at this was that he would make big bets on people. One talented finance individual was brought from Continental Europe to run an SAP implementation, then to the head-of-strategy role, then to a COO-type role in Europe, and finally to be president of the China businesses. He was being groomed for the company's CFO role, and these moves were intended to build his experience base. Big bets take courage, but most pay off.

Key Components of Succession Planning

It's best to have a somewhat formal approach to succession planning in order to focus the right level of attention on the activity. After all, you're laying out the key components that need to be implemented for the business to thrive in the future. Data should be gathered, people should be engaged in discussions, summaries or plans should be documented, and discussions should be organized.

Sometimes, during this work, terminology can be confusing. In particular, people are often confused about the difference between top-talent and high-potential employees. Here are common definitions I've used in the past:

- *Top talents* are those who generate great results and have the ability to continue to do so. They assume more responsibility, and it would be a significant loss if they left the company.

- *High potentials* are those with the ability to assume great scope in terms of complexity, breadth, and scale, and who typically can move up in the organization one or two levels over time.

The top-talent pool may include high potentials, but not everyone in the top-talent pool is a high potential. The intent is to distinguish one from another to be able to invest appropriately. Developmental efforts for people who have big runways in front of them and lots of potential should be different from those who are great but will continue to do largely similar work.

Tools and Frameworks

Below are the most valuable tools and frameworks to help you prepare for good succession planning that I've found in my many years of work in this area. They should prompt extensive discussions and help you develop robust plans. The work should be very realistic, actual, and true. Succession planning is often one of the biggest wastes of organizational time because of how poorly it's done and managed. It's also one of the most frustrating activities for employees, and that's all unnecessary.

Strategic Frameworks
Strategic frameworks are one-page summaries of the strategic priorities of the organization over the next three to five years. They galvanize people to organize their thinking at the start of a discussion.

Frameworks should include specific plans for mergers and acquisitions work, organic growth, new markets, etc.

Placemats

Placemats are one-page summaries of the leadership team. They serve as a quick reference. Often they include organizational charts with names, titles, promotability ratings, and timing on promotability:

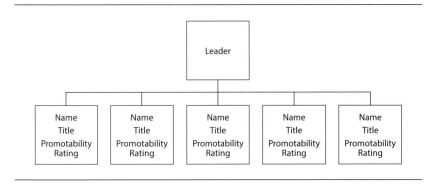

Stack Ranks

Stack ranks are listings of the most-important to least-important people on the organizational chart. Here's a series of questions you need to ask to create your stack rank: Who is the most valuable member of your team? Who's the next most valuable? The next? Your answers should determine what investments should be made in your team members.

Stack Rank
1. Patt
2. Ray
3. Beth
4. Rick
5. Kate
6. Linda
7. Cindy
8. Steve
9. Reen
10. Kim

Here are two ways to think about stack ranks. First, if you were on the playground picking a team from scratch, who would you select first because they have the most to offer? Who would you select next? A second way to think about how to create a stack rank is to consider it as if you were in a boat and it was taking on water and someone had to go overboard for everyone to survive, who would go first? Who would go next? This may seem harsh, but you need to look at the talent with a critical eye so you can carry on your duties as a steward of the company. At the same time, being at the bottom of a stack rank doesn't mean the employee is bad. Ranking is an exercise in prioritizing even though sometimes all of the employees are good. In the end, though, the employees don't all have the same value to the business. If you have to choose who to invest in or who to reward you want to make sure the people most important to the business are first in line.

People often freak out about stack ranks. Managers don't like doing them, and employees worry about them. I say toughen up. If an employee doesn't want to be at the bottom of a stack rank, they should do something about it. If managers don't want to make hard calls to identify the most valuable members of the team, they shouldn't be managing. Business is tough, and leaders need to be tough as well.

High Potentials Development Plans
Outline for your high potentials what their next move is and the move after that. Include timing on the moves, development activities, and a rating of the level of risk they pose in terms of leaving the company:

High Potential Name	Next Move & Timing	Second Move & Timing	Retention Risk Hi, Med, Lo	Development Activities

Functional Scorecards
Functional scorecards are useful for grading the various functions within a division or company. Outline overall strengths and areas for improvement:

Overall Grade on Talent for XYZ Function: _____	
Strengths	Areas to Improve

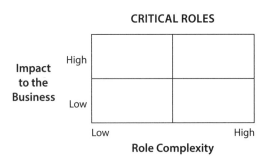

Exhibit 9-1. Chart your critical roles based on their complexity and how much they impact the business. Critical roles will usually be found in the upper right quadrant.

Chart your plans for critical roles to make sure they are guarded against vacancy (see Exhibit 9-1). What's a critical role? Use these questions to help you determine which roles are truly critical:

- Does the position significantly impact business results?
- Is the person in the position driving tremendous growth?
- Is the role large and complex?
- Is the skill set difficult to get in the marketplace or difficult to develop?
- If you put the wrong person in the role, what are the ramifications and risks?

Once you determine which roles are critical, determine your succession plan for those roles (see Exhibit 9-2).

Top Talents Profiles

You should keep a profile on each of the people in your top talent pool. These profiles should include specifics about their history, strengths, developmental areas, promotability, mobility, languages, etc. The profiles should serve as briefs on the individuals and be made known to the decision-making leaders.

Use the Data

While completing these forms may seem like a lot of work (compared to just having conversations), it's a great practice to have this informa-

POSITION & PERSON IN ROLE Years in Role Anticipated Move Date	POTENTIAL SUCCESSORS		
	Readiness	Name	Title
	Ready Now		
	Ready 1-2 yrs		
	Ready 3-5 yrs		
	Ready Now		
	Ready 1-2 yrs		
	Ready 3-5 yrs		
	Ready Now		
	Ready 1-2 yrs		
	Ready 3-5 yrs		

Exhibit 9-2. Use this chart to help you determine your succession plan.

tion on paper for several reasons. First, it establishes clarity because everyone sees the same information. Second, it's a great tool for your succession planners or teams to use for planning or to provide to the organization to support their succession planning efforts.

Darcie Zeliesko used to work for me as a talent development leader. Darcie lived and breathed succession planning. She offers this perspective: "Consider succession planning very critical to the success of any organization. The most challenging part of engaging in the process is gathering the data, especially in a global company. The rules of engagement should be to gather the least amount of data to help you make the very best decisions and to ensure you have built in a review process to keep it alive throughout the year. I have returned to the data from the annual process time and time again, and I'm always thankful to have that information to make educated decisions on talent, especially in other parts of the world where I may not have been close to the talent. It is a necessary process, but be sure to simplify where you can and ensure you keep it alive throughout the year since it is a huge effort. This will encourage your leadership teams to understand the value year after year. In addition to this, creating transparency and accountability in the process is key to its success.

Do I tell a leader where they stand? Absolutely yes! Many companies or leaders are fearful of giving feedback."

A comprehensive process and set of tools provide good data so you can do the analytics to determine trends and needs.

Lorrina Eastman was a master at using succession-planning data. "When I was responsible for succession planning at a Fortune 100 company, my team and I created a Health of the Bench summary, which was an objective and quantitative analysis of each line of business's or function's talent bench. We analyzed health of the bench by summarizing data such as replacement charts (including the number of unique, ready-now candidates), diversity of replacement charts and talent, depth of the talent pool, amount of talent churn within the organization, progress-developing talent, etc. The outcomes captured the interest of the business leaders and were also very helpful in creating headlines that we shared with the board of directors (it also sent a strong message to the board that we had a strong read on talent within the organization and where there were opportunities). Focus on discussion of talent and creating accountability for development. Fancy templates and systems are great enablers but are nice-to-haves versus essential. What matters most is that leaders are committed to routinely discussing their talent and actively supporting their development."

Determining Promotability

One of the most difficult elements in people planning for the future is figuring out who has more runway in front of them: Who is promotable? Who is good enough to do more? Can they do more only in terms of volume, or can they handle complexity? There are several ways organizations determine promotability, and here are two examples.

One framework becoming popular for determining promotability is using learning agility as a measure of how far a person can go long-term. The Center for Creative Leadership (CCL), a development house, has created an assessment that can be used as a predictor of ability to be stretched and do more. You can employ this framework and assessment to look at an individual's mental agility, results agility, people agility, and change agility and use the results to predict whether they could handle a bigger workload and more complex responsibilities in the future.

Another way to determine promotability is to have roundtable discussions with leaders who have seen the employees being discussed in action over time. Possible questions you can use to drive these discussions include: Does this person currently have the capability to work anywhere in the organization? To have significant decision-making responsibilities? To set strategy? To lead change?

A typical tool used to evaluate promotability is a nine-box grid you use to rate potential along the bottom and performance along the left hand side.

Looking at how a person has performed typically over the last three years and thinking about what they might do in the future, leaders sort names into the nine boxes. Based on where the names land, the plan is to promote and develop, keep as is, or eliminate.

CCL is renowned for its expertise in developing people, especially leaders. The company publishes insightful research and has custom and open-enrollment programs across a number of platforms. Because of CCL's proven success many talent professionals have used its methodologies. Lorrina Eastman has spent years in talent development and is currently a vice president at Catalyst. "I am a big fan of CCL's high-potential research, which revealed that the majority of high potentials are not actually high potential because they lack either the ambition or engagement. I have used their three-pronged model for identifying high potentials with multiple clients and have always found it to be a helpful tool."

Doreen Diaz, a talent-development executive I've worked with, has a great framework that pulls this all together and guides me to this day: "Know the talent, know the role, develop the talent, move the talent."

Roles and Responsibilities

This work on determining promotability should involve several parties. Managers should be working with their employees to understand what's important to the employees in terms of their career development, and they should be keeping key employee data updated. HR should be collecting information in preparation for leadership discussions. Leaders should plan for conversations with each other to determine answers to key organizational development questions.

Common Pitfalls of Succession Planning

Be careful to avoid the following traps when doing this work:

- Hoarding talent. Talent has to be viewed as a shared resource. Managers who are not willing to give up their talent for the good of the company are the kiss of death for good succession plans. *This is the single biggest obstacle to good talent development – managers won't give up their talent.* Without a shared commitment, succession planning and career development efforts are wasted efforts.

- Identifying someone as ready now who is actually not ready or not willing to make a change.

- Identifying someone as mobile who actually won't move when pressed.

- Identifying someone as ready in one to two years for five years in a row (that math doesn't work).

- Not sharing feedback from succession plans with employees.

- Not executing the plans.

- Using the same person on all succession charts. Succession charts should include a wide variety of names inside and outside a division, inside and outside an organization. Managers have an ongoing responsibility for identifying potential talent to bring in from outside the company.

- Worrying about offending someone by not including him or her in a succession plan or by not listing their role on the list of critical roles. Succession planning isn't a beauty contest or a soccer game where everyone gets a trophy. This is about the long-term health of the organization, where leadership courage and objectivity are the tickets for entry into the conversation.

- Not putting people into stretch assignments, waiting until they're "ready." Great companies put people into jobs before they're ready. Every one of the leaders I spoke with who would be classified as very successful had been put into roles that were a stretch for them. In reflecting on this, they pointed out that good companies make this a habit and have sustainable talent pools, while companies that don't do this and are cautious are not ones from which they try to steal talent.

- Not supporting employees in roles that are stretches for them. The person leaving the role and the person managing the employee in the stretch assignment should, as part of their performance goals, help ensure that the employee coming into the role will be successful.

- Not making big bets on people. I've had exposure to several great CEOs who did this well. You need to take and manage the risk to get tremendous results.

Make sure succession-planning time is used productively. I've worked with a CEO who held a three-day meeting to review the succession plans of each business. When I first began working with his team, he would storm out when the conversation became too tactical. While

I don't condone this type of behavior, it did send a message to his team that the meeting wasn't worth his time, which was his intent. People evolved their presentations to focus on the strategic direction of the business and the skills and capabilities needed for the future. The CEO was highly engaged in subsequent conversations as a result.

During one of these sessions, the president of the United Kingdom business made a proposal that a think tank was needed in the business. The business had been in existence for a long time, and to achieve growth they needed revolutionary ideas. He used this succession-planning meeting to discuss this investment in people. It wasn't an easy conversation, and the CEO told the president he was taking a big risk. The president assumed the responsibility and went with it. It afforded talent a number of opportunities to stretch and grow and, most importantly, it was created to drive business growth. The result was tremendous growth for that business, and the think tank approach was adopted by several other businesses in the company. These are exactly the types of conversations and ideas that should evolve in these types of meetings and what all the effort should be able to attain.

Systematic, Long-Term Development

Long-term development often takes a concerted effort. The best way to develop top talent and future leaders is for a company to create solutions from the top that have senior-level engagement.

When I was at Hasbro, we partnered with Tuck Business School to create a development program for senior leaders. It was an immersion experience in Hanover, New Hampshire, where leaders came from around the world to spend time with learned professors. Additionally, our chairman of the board, Alan Hassenfeld, would spend the entire time with the group underscoring key messages and being available for breakfast, lunch, and dinner to assess the talent and provide coaching.

At another company we had several solutions. One was the CEO Academy, which involved the CEO, the head of HR, and me. We spent three days with nine participants from around the world. Talk about a commitment. It was a great opportunity to provide clarity about leadership expectations and to get to know the talent.

We also created a Functional Leader Program. This was a year-long program that consisted of a week of classroom work that occurred on a different continent every quarter, culminating in an action-learning experience during the last quarter. The program was global and divided its focus between leading self, leading others, and leading the business. People were nominated by business unit presidents and HR leaders to take part in the program, and the CEO, the chief people officer, and I made final attendance decisions. The program had heavy senior-leader involvement, and it fundamentally changed lives. This intentional development over time made a big difference in our talent pool.

Many people I know are fans of structured assignments. Paul Farmer, an HR and talent professional, has used them extensively. "I have had tremendous success creating a Leadership Development Rotation Program consisting of six-month, structured assignments that were measured and had leader buy-in, support, and engagement. They included structured coaching and feedback, which led to the creation of a leadership pipeline still used five years later."

Some leaders have employed long-term development efforts for individuals. A respected global senior leader I've worked with, Albert Moncau, is terrific at it. Here's an example: "What comes to my mind is the development of a key account manager in France who, after six years, became managing director of the South West Region for that same company. We basically used the standard tools (360 feedback and performance appraisals) to identify and select, one, the personal career goals and, two, the areas of improvement to be able to attain those goals. Once that was clear, we gave this person different on-the-job challenges to develop those weak skills and also new ones. As an example, he led the acquisition process from a commercial perspective, which developed his capability to own and believe in businesses and people he didn't know, to trust them as well, and to be able to adapt to different ways of doing business in order to get the maximum from his team. We did something similar when giving him the marketing lead on top of his sales lead, developing in him the mindset of one common team with common beliefs, and also putting him on a higher ladder of the organization, which forced him to bring solutions to the table rather than problems. And finally he successfully replaced me when I moved." What's neat about this quote is that Moncau is referring to someone I spoke about previously in this book as an example of a tremendous leader.

Developmental efforts don't need to be confined to people who work directly for you. Sometimes identifying talent in other areas and, with permission, using that employee as part of your work is a great opportunity for people to develop new skills.

One of the best examples of this is a woman we'll call Sharon who came to work for me. When Sharon approached me, she was working on redesigning the worldwide product development process. She had been in marketing, had worked on the line in manufacturing, and had worked in packaging and other areas. She had no people-development experience. She expressed interest in my area and asked if she could help out to learn more about it. At the time I was rolling out sexual harassment training and corporate conduct training across the organization. The training model I was using paired a line person with an HR person to facilitate the training so they could have relevant conversations with employees about these important topics. I partnered Sharon with an HR person to give her a people-development opportunity.

She was very good. She wasn't great yet. I gave her some coaching on presenting and used her again when I rolled out a highly interactive diversity-training module across the company. It was a fun and engaging module that allowed people to have deeper conversations if that's what the group wanted. I used a co-facilitation model for this program as well. Sharon did really well. Her style was a great match for this content. People felt safe around her. She was a very "real" person.

I had an opening on my team and Sharon applied for it. She didn't get the job. At the time, I needed someone who had more in-depth people development and instructional design experience, and I hired someone from outside the company. It was probably the wrong decision on my part but the right decision in terms of its impact on Sharon. It made her angry. I was clear in my feedback about what was missing and what I needed to see to consider her for a future opportunity. I worked with her on these areas. When there was another opening on my team, she applied and was the perfect choice. Getting the message that she wasn't ready, with clarity about what was missing along with coaching to help her close the gap, resulted in her channeling her efforts toward improvement. She came to work with me at two more companies where she was held in very high regard. She's appreciated for her hard work, her intelligence, her willingness to take feedback and apply it, and her ability to get things done. She's a global superstar on any team she's part of. And it all started with her dropping by my office to offer her services because she was interested in learning something new.

If you find people outside your team who have more capacity and capability than they're using in their current jobs, use them. It's just good business sense, as we've seen with Sharon. Navigating that move can be a bit tricky, however. Here's a recommended approach on how to go about doing it:

- First, ask the person if they've spoken to their manager about it. If they haven't, they need to.

- Once that's done, sit down with the person to see what they're interested in helping with, what their strengths and developmental areas are, and what they hope to get out of the experience. They should be getting something back for assisting, and I'm an advocate of helping people develop through a process such as this.

- Following this conversation, you should have a conversation with the person's manager to make sure they're on board and that you understand any limitations.

- Once this is done, set some expectations about where and when the person can help, and determine whether they have the skills and resources to do the work immediately.

- Coach, provide feedback, and demonstrate appreciation throughout your time together.

This work takes commitment and perseverance. A talented financial services executive experienced this for himself and his direct reports. As he matured over time and learned about himself and others, he found that persistence was important. "The process takes time and is much like developing new habits. You need to have expectations that change will be gradual, and for it to stick you need to allow for course corrections and continuous feedback and training."

I'm an optimist. My parents raised me to believe that if I wanted to achieve something I could do it. Realism has seeped in along the way, but overall this is a mindset that's gotten me pretty far. John F. Kennedy said, "We will put a man on the moon in ten years," while the Russians, with their advanced space program, hadn't done that, and the United States barely had a space program. A wise professor, Vijay Govindarajan, once said in relation to this quote, "If you shoot for the moon, you might at least hit the top of the tree. If you shoot for the top of the tree, you may hit the first branch. There's power in shooting for the moon." Vijay is an amazing educator. I strongly recommend that you get to know more about Vijay and his work. He has authored books on strategy, globalization, and other areas that are well worth reading.

The Chapter's Big Ideas

- Succession planning and career development both take into consideration the strategic direction of the company and the employee's needs and interests, but which one is a primary focus depends on whether you are the employee (career development) or the company (succession planning).
- Top talents are those who generate great results and have the ability to continue to do so. They assume more responsibility, and it would be a significant loss if they left the company.

- High potentials are those with the ability to assume great scope in terms of complexity, breadth, and scale of the work they could do and who typically can move up the organization one or two levels over time. The top-talent pool may include high potentials, but not everyone in the top-talent pool has high potential.

- There are a number of tools and frameworks available to help you do succession planning. Determine what you need to help drive decision making and action and research your options. Simplicity is key.

- People get freaky about stack ranks, but they are powerful tools – use them. But remember, the form is the conduit, not the destination.

- Forms can be a great place to capture data for future use, such as in developing training plans or considering future job openings. A form is intended to help organize your thinking and act as a communication tool.

- There are a number of ways companies do succession planning incorrectly. Understand the pitfalls and make sure you aren't repeating other people's mistakes.

- Empowering senior leaders makes for powerful succession planning efforts.

- Top leaders deliver great results and are known for developing people. This development should happen at all levels.

- Managers should consider themselves ineligible for another role until they've developed a succession plan for their current role. Succession planning should happen at all levels of the organization.

- There are many people who feel underutilized and under-challenged in their organizations. Look to tap into these people and trade developing them for an extra set of hands. Be sure to get permission from their manager.

- Succession planning is important for all kinds of companies (large, small, public, private), all functions, and ideally is done at all organizational levels for greatest impact.

SUCCESSION PLANNING ASSESSMENT

On a scale of 1 to 10, with 1 being not at all and 10 being at an industry standard level, rate your organization on the following questions:

	LOW 1 2 3 4 5 6 7 8	HIGH 9 10
1. How public is the succession planning process in your organization?	☐ ☐ ☐ ☐ ☐ ☐ ☐ ☐	☐ ☐
2. How accountable are managers in the succession planning process?	☐ ☐ ☐ ☐ ☐ ☐ ☐ ☐	☐ ☐
3. How much appropriate feedback needed for their development is provided to employees from succession planning efforts?	☐ ☐ ☐ ☐ ☐ ☐ ☐ ☐	☐ ☐
4. How often are efforts made specifically to develop and retain high potentials?	☐ ☐ ☐ ☐ ☐ ☐ ☐ ☐	☐ ☐
5. How widely are stack ranks used?	☐ ☐ ☐ ☐ ☐ ☐ ☐ ☐	☐ ☐
6. How many people in your organization are ready for a new challenge?	☐ ☐ ☐ ☐ ☐ ☐ ☐ ☐	☐ ☐
7. How widely known and defined are the leadership philosophies of the company?	☐ ☐ ☐ ☐ ☐ ☐ ☐ ☐	☐ ☐
8. How many people in your organization would say that they have more capacity and capability?	☐ ☐ ☐ ☐ ☐ ☐ ☐ ☐	☐ ☐
9. How accurate are succession plans, and how often are they executed against when a position opens up?	☐ ☐ ☐ ☐ ☐ ☐ ☐ ☐	☐ ☐
10. How willing are leaders to work together for the betterment of the organization and to do things such as give up top talent for roles they are needed for or to develop them?	☐ ☐ ☐ ☐ ☐ ☐ ☐ ☐	☐ ☐

SUCCESSION PLANNING ACTION STEPS

For anything you rated less than 9, what are you going to do about it?

Question #	Actions to Take	Timeframe	People to Involve

CHAPTER TEN

Career Development

CAREER PLANNING AND DEVELOPMENT are closely linked to individual development planning and succession planning. Decisions and plans made during succession planning efforts should be based on good input from career planning conversations that should happen with employees prior to the succession planning discussions. Output from career and succession planning discussions should be translated into goals and actions and recorded in employees' individual development plans.

For career planning and development to work, you need an infrastructure that supports them. The company must be committed to a culture of developing and advancing people so moves can actually happen. Managers are responsible for the discussions and helping employees get on the road to their next opportunities; the company needs to set expectations for this to happen. This is a big gap in most companies. Companies derail in this area by not taking risks, not holding managers accountable for the advancement of their talent, and not looking at the individuals as utility players who can be used in many places. Companies need to wrestle with some key questions, and the leadership team needs to drive the corresponding behaviors to help create this culture:

- What is our philosophy about how long a person should be in a job, and if they pass that mark, what are we willing to do about it?

- What is the soonest someone can leave a job?

- What is the consequence for leaders who don't develop their talent?

- How will we determine if people are good and standardize our definition of good so it's equitable?

- What do we think about temporary assignments? Global assignments? Are our relocation policies and practices competitive?

- Who is accountable for helping people in new, significantly bigger, and different roles to be successful?

Agreement among the management team, with behaviors that support their beliefs, will result in a company that has a sustainable pipeline of talent.

Even if the environment is conducive to career development, career planning is still difficult for managers to do. Here are some of the reasons I've heard:

- Managers don't want to make promises they can't keep.

- Managers don't think they're insightful enough to be able to help chart out a course for someone.

- Managers feel threatened.

Employees expect to be invested in and developed. They don't expect to start a job and five years later be in the same job with the same skills doing the same work. Managers should work themselves out of a job. I've always had this mindset, and it has served me well as a manager with my various teams and as a professional growing up through the ranks. While I may be in love with my current job, I know that won't be the case forever. I know I will eventually outgrow the job or become bored. I want to be ready to take advantage of other growth opportunities as they come down the pike. The only way I can do that is if there are strong successors and a sustainable model, processes, and tools in place so my leaders can imagine the work going on without me.

Antonio Nunez has been a successful general manager in Venezuela, an incredibly difficult market. He has successfully handled career development even with the ever-changing constraints and conditions in that country. Antonio said, "Developing a successor is the most challenging and can be the most confusing process. 'You need to develop a backup before moving forward in the organization.' 'You need to have your successor up and ready prior to your next promotion.' 'There are no opportunities in the company unless you develop your substitute.' I heard these messages many times before – they are clear, fair, and they sound great. But if there are no plans agreed to between leader and organization, as simple as sincere and trustful talks, these messages can become smoking bombs on your route to grow professionally and confusing signals that may interfere with your performance. Organizations clearly need to identify when it is the right time to let talent move forward."

Philosophy is important, but planning and action are more important for career development to be successful. Managers need to get their own house in order mentally, skill-wise, and performance-wise before they try to help their employees with career development.

What's the worst-case scenario? You develop someone and they leave? They're likely to leave if you don't develop them. You develop them and they're pushing for your job? Good. That means you have a strong member of your team ready to help drive the business forward. You give them bad advice on where and how to develop? Do research, get other people's opinions, and know that development comes in a lot of ways. Don't have the answers? Get them.

Some managers feel uncomfortable dealing with employees who have ambitions that go beyond their capability (in the manager's judgment). Here are some guidelines on how to be more comfortable handling those situations:

- Work with the employee to lay out a profile of the skills, experience, and knowledge needed to be successful in a given role. Have them map their current competencies to that profile to determine the gap they need to close. Discuss what's necessary for them to do in order to close that gap and how realistic it is that they'll be able to.

- Help the employee connect with people who are already in the role they'd like to have, and interview those people about how they got the role, what the role is like, and what the employee would need to do to get there.

Ground Rules

For effective career planning discussions to be successful, some ground rules are needed. Here are some suggestions:

- Employees have careers, organizations don't. The career planning process is driven and owned by the employees. Managers are supporting players.

- If employees choose to be delusional about their skill sets, let them. You can't force them to change their minds. While encouraging them to create a profile on the desired job and assess themselves against that profile, you can provide your input about how they're lining up with a fact-based response.

- Don't be discouraging. Be positive and encouraging.

- Stress that there are no guarantees and that your role is to help open doors and explore ideas.

- Be honest as to what you perceive their constraints to be, and ask what they perceive their constraints to be. Brainstorm with employees about constraints and help them test out the reality and firmness of their constraints. (Constraints could be family, timing, geography, skill or knowledge areas, health, or other limitations.)

- Think in terms of the following:
  - What additional responsibilities can I give this person to stretch them or help them attain their goals?
  - What skills or knowledge do they need, and what role can I play in helping them develop these?

If employees are going to have career planning conversations for the first time, give them questions to think about in preparation:

- What types of responsibilities do you like?
- How and where have you been successful in using your skills, knowledge, and experience in the past?
- What type of position would you like next?
- What are your long-term hopes and dreams?
- Do you have any strong preferences (likes and dislikes) that might factor into a future role?
- Do you have any limitations that would prevent you from taking a role?
- What are the developmental areas that you're working on and still need to work on in your opinion?

Employees might come to career planning sessions with their own questions, such as:

- Where can I go from here?
- How do I get from where I am to my next role and when?
- I like my job. How do I stay here?
- Why didn't I get the last promotion?
- I've seen a job I want to apply for. What do I do?
- Where do you see me going long-term?
- How do I get your job?

- What's the biggest challenge standing in my way?

- Is there anything you think about me or know about me that I don't know?

Think short- and long-term when it comes to career development. An IDP should cover the next twelve months, while a career plan should have horizons of three, five, and ten years.

Work Career Development and Succession Planning Together

When an employee's desires intersect with the company growth plans, managers have a tremendous opportunity to influence the developmental efforts of that individual. Additionally, homegrown leaders are powerful because they understand the messaging and strategic direction of the company already.

There are many creative things you as a manager can do to develop your team members. A strong leader I've worked with, Jan Kruise, was vigilant about stretching and developing his team. He often moved them into various roles to give them cross-functional exposure and to further develop their thinking.

Another executive I've worked with, David Bailin, was excellent at thinking through the possibilities of how to stretch people, and he gave them major opportunities. He used changing times, such as during the consolidation of teams resulting from a merger, to test people and put them into new roles or new work. His commitment to do this created strong followership from his team.

There are valuable career development assessment tools available to help employees sort through some ideas if they're struggling. The Sheine Career Anchors and the Career Interest Profiler are two such examples. There are also software solutions that help this process. A friend of mine, the chief human resources officer at MasterCard, has had success with a particular tool: "We have had great success in using a concept called Smart Moves and Smart Steps. Focus was on career development. Smart Moves focused on how you make lateral career moves to enhance your career to prepare you for future leadership or larger roles. Often we tend to always think about the next promotion. Smart Steps was a concept for leaders to create shadow experiences of all types to give employees the opportunity to develop."

Don't expect the career planning process to follow a straight line, regardless of the quality of the conversations you've had. A little thing called life tends to get in the way. A customer business management executive, Jon Rocco Mccan, believes in supporting his direct reports' career planning efforts. "Get as much detail to best understand what they want out of their career and work on how to accomplish this in your company's current environment. Far too often people look at career pathing as linear when, in fact, a zigzag approach is far better and makes you a more well-rounded person."

Sometimes what an employee wants isn't what you want. I've worked with a talented HR person in Asia, Laurent Low. He was exceptional on so many levels and would have been a great potential successor for the top HR role in the company. However, based on the age of his children and where he saw himself (helping emerging market companies grow), he wasn't a viable candidate. A peer of Laurent's at the time, Nigel Perry, was also a strong potential successor. He was interested in advancing his career, so he chose to challenge himself by becoming the head of HR for the U.S. business as a way to test his potential for success in the top HR job. This is an example of why career development needs to be employee-driven. It takes aggressive work and trade-offs. Supporting your employees' efforts to align with organizational needs is the best approach you can take to help your employees be successful. Sometimes, even by giving your full support to your employee's career development, you still won't be able to keep top talent. Meg Whitman was running the Playskool division for us at Hasbro when she received the call to become CEO of a small, unknown business called eBay. Within days of her arrival eBay went public, and the rest is history. Sometimes it's better for employees to pursue opportunities outside the organization. Wish those people well and go back to doing great development work with your existing high-potential population.

The Chapter's Big Ideas

- Decisions and plans made during succession planning should be based on input from good career planning conversations with employees.

- Outputs from career- and succession-planning conversations should be translated into employees' IDPs.

- Managers are often unskilled and insecure in the career development area, providing poor career development support to their employees.

- The best career development support a company can provide employees is to have a good infrastructure for moving into and out of roles.

- Employees have careers, companies don't, so career development should be employee-driven and manager- and company-supported.

- Employees should be trying to work themselves out of their job from the day they start as a way to build a sustainable talent pipeline.

- A supportive mindset from managers is needed, but specific action plans are required for career development to work.

- A career development assessment might be a good resource for an employee in sorting through his or her interests and options.

CAREER DEVELOPMENT ASSESSMENT

On a scale of 1 to 10, with 1 being not at all and 10 being at an industry standard level, rate your organization on the following questions:	LOW 1 2 3 4 5 6 7 8 9 HIGH 10
1. How often are career development conversations conducted in your organization?	☐ ☐ ☐ ☐ ☐ ☐ ☐ ☐ ☐ ☐
2. How tightly linked are career development conversations to succession planning and individual development planning?	☐ ☐ ☐ ☐ ☐ ☐ ☐ ☐ ☐ ☐
3. How accountable are managers for developing successors?	☐ ☐ ☐ ☐ ☐ ☐ ☐ ☐ ☐ ☐
4. How accountable are managers for the career development of their team members?	☐ ☐ ☐ ☐ ☐ ☐ ☐ ☐ ☐ ☐
5. How empowered do employees feel in raising career development as a topic and navigating their way through the organization?	☐ ☐ ☐ ☐ ☐ ☐ ☐ ☐ ☐ ☐
6. How well defined and known is the company's philosophy on development, such as how long someone should be in a role?	☐ ☐ ☐ ☐ ☐ ☐ ☐ ☐ ☐ ☐
7. How familiar are managers with tools to support employees' thinking about career development?	☐ ☐ ☐ ☐ ☐ ☐ ☐ ☐ ☐ ☐

SUCCESSION PLANNING ACTION STEPS

For anything you rated less than 9, what are you going to do about it?

Question #	Actions to Take	Timeframe	People to Involve

CHAPTER ELEVEN

Coaching and Feedback

W<small>E ARE ABOUT TO COVER</small> one of my favorite talent management topics – coaching and feedback. I believe in this topic so deeply that I struggled to decide where to place this chapter in the book. I wanted it to go at the beginning, middle, and end because coaching and feedback make or break the talent management efforts discussed earlier in this book. Good coaching and feedback skills are the biggest differentiators of great leaders (and high performers in general). If you're good at coaching, I suggest that you read through this chapter for additional ideas to make you even better. If you aren't so great at coaching, get reading!

First, to clarify and distinguish between coaching and feedback, let's define them. I think of coaching as simply helping someone reach a new level. Coaching can be short-term or long-term. It can be task-related, behavior-related, career-related, performance-related … you name it. Coaching is who you are, not something you do. It's a mindset as much as it's a skill set. Feedback is giving input on something that's happened. Feedback is a gift. It should be given with the purest intent. If you're just getting something off your chest, that's not feedback. That's venting, and it has consequences, so be aware of what you're doing. But since feedback is a gift, the receiver can choose to use it or not.

Coaching

Why is it that we readily accept the notion of coaching in athletics but not in the workplace? Everyone expects a top golfer or tennis player to work with a coach. Everyone finds it acceptable to see a coach as part of a football game. But most leaders don't provide coaching, and most employees don't demand it.

The Corporate Leadership Council, a successful think tank and research organization, has researched the value of coaching. They have found that coaching is a top driver of employee performance and retention. They learned that it's in the top five of preferred developmental interventions and ranks above any other formal program.

Now that the reasons for coaching are clear, let's get down to understanding it. There are two requirements in coaching – skill and will. Will is essential. You've got to be willing to commit yourself to someone else and his or her success. Skill at coaching is also essential. Successful coaching isn't hard work – it just requires robust dialogue, good instruction, practice, commitment to change, good feedback skills, and a genuine interest.

Coaching is a head, heart, and guts activity, and it encompasses some essential elements:

1. You must have a genuine interest in seeing people improve and succeed. If you ask people to think about someone in their lives who played a significant role as a coach, what you'll hear, time and time again, is that that person cared about his or her success. Even in brief interactions, brief coaching moments, you can feel if someone cares. That caring matters and makes a big difference.

2. A good coach is accomplished at dialogue. That back and forth exchange – providing and seeking input – is necessary in a coaching situation. Both parties should be seeking to understand and be understood.

3. A good coach is able to break subjects down to their essentials to provide clear instruction. Simplicity is key. If not

an expert in the subject, a coach should bring in others who are to provide instruction.

4. A coach values and promotes practice. A coach needs to be able to create a safe environment where people can practice. If people are worried about having to be perfect from the start, then learning is compromised.

5. A coach has to believe that change is important and be able to help people understand why change is important to their success.

6. Being able to provide feedback that's useful, understandable, relevant, and packaged in a way that's palatable is a key skill in a coach's skill set. We'll discuss feedback in more detail later.

Effective coaching consists of four steps:

1. Help employees understand their current situation regarding an issue and why it's important to address it.

2. Help employees understand how to change their situation.

3. Help employees practice.

4. Let employees know how they did in addressing the issue.

Step #1

Help employees understand their current situation regarding an issue and why it's important to address it.

Comparison and context are important. Specificity is essential. All coaching should start by identifying the issue at hand. An example of a behavioral issue could be that an employee is poor at delivering presentations. A performance example could be that they haven't delivered their number three quarters in a row. A development example could be that they want to improve their decision-making skills.

If you don't fully understand the situation, probe further first. If it's something someone has been working on for a period of time, make sure you understand where he or she is and what's been done about the issue. Some questions you could ask are:

- What are you doing now?

- What have you tried previously?

- What advice have you received so far?

- What results have you seen from these efforts?

- What's stopping you from being better?

Helping someone understand how much something needs to be different is essential for that person to be able to achieve a new level of success. That's true whether the issue is performance or behavior. You wouldn't tell a salesperson who didn't hit their number that they need to deliver more without telling them how much more. You wouldn't tell an employee who was a poor presenter that they need to improve their presentation skills without telling them how much they need to improve or where. (Some managers probably would, but lack of specificity makes success unlikely.)

If an employee has been performing a task for some time, they usually have internally calibrated how much effort feels appropriate to complete the task. Let's consider our presentation skills example. If someone is working on projecting their voice to improve their presentations, projecting it as little as 5 percent more might feel like a significant change, and they'll be a bit uncomfortable in doing it. Why? Because their internal schema tells them that's not how they presented in the past, and any change will cause discomfort. But if the employee actually needs to project 50 percent more to present well, then they need to make a huge change, and they need to be told that their expectations are off and that their level of discomfort might be significant. That's where good coaching comes into play.

Helping someone understand why a change is necessary engenders commitment. If people understand why, they're more likely to own the change and make it last. Every time I coach someone about understanding the impact of the presence or absence of a behavior, and what the trickle-down effect would be as a result, they're much more willing to change.

In this first step, getting a verbal contract on your employee's expectations is important. While you don't want to pepper people with rapid-fire, intimidating questions, you want to be sure you get answers to the following questions, overtly or subtly, so you understand the situation:

- What do you want to achieve?

- What does success look like?

- Who is involved? Who are the stakeholders in this?

- What do you expect of me?

- What is your timeframe?

- How big of a stretch is this for you?

Step #2

Help employees understand how to change their situation.

The best coaches wear many hats. There are some schools of thought that say coaches don't tell and don't teach but rather lead people through a process of self-discovery to help them improve. I had a long battle with colleagues in a U.K. business previously about this approach because I don't agree with it. While it's a good strategy to be used at times, other strategies may be required depending on the situation.

Teaching is one technique a good coach can draw upon to help employees improve. The sooner someone can internalize what they're doing and what needs to change, the easier and quicker the adjustment. But if someone has been having a tough time making decisions, they may need to be taught different strategies on how to make decisions. Sometimes a coach has to be a teacher. Sometimes, depending upon the situation, a coach might also need to actually tell someone how to do something, or actually do it for them, if they don't know how to or aren't seeing the situation clearly.

The more tools a coach has to draw upon, the better the coach's ability to positively influence the desired outcome. There are many ways to help someone improve. The coaching strategy should vary based on the situation or the employee. Some of these coaching strategies are: asking, listening, directing, giving feedback, practicing, connecting with resources, teaching, and sharing/storytelling.

Asking

A big component of my coaching style is to ask open-ended questions. Asking questions does several things: it prompts the discussion, it puts the responsibility on the other person, it teaches them to reflect, which helps them get to self-management faster, it diffuses the emotion surrounding the situation, and it gives you, the manager, time to think and gain insight into what the other person is thinking. Some examples of open-ended questions to consider using are:

- How would you …?
- What do you think about …?
- Tell me about …?
- What was your reasoning …?
- Help me understand …?

Make sure your questioning approach isn't aggressive. The intent is not to put people on the ropes in answering your questions and make them defensive. The intent is to understand and to help them reflect. Engagement is the goal. Avoid judgmental language in your exchanges since that will shut down the conversation or redirect it in a way that's not consistent with achieving the desired outcome. Good examples of judgmental language are "You shouldn't be so foolish" or "You're a poor team player and need to get better."

Listening

As adults in the workforce, we've been conditioned to tell, and that makes it difficult to listen. Many times when it appears that we're listening, we're actually figuring out what we need to tell the person when they're done speaking, which creates communication issues. As a coach, listening to the person to understand the situation and how that person is feeling about it will give you a big advantage in helping them deal with the issue. As a coach, you should be listening to:

- Yourself – While listening, you most likely have a conversation going on in your head pertaining to the conversation at hand as well as others. We all home in on what interests us and relates to us. It's natural to consciously or unconsciously do this, particularly on points that resonate with you. But doing this blocks you from hearing or seeing all aspects of the conversation. Mentally shutting off those other conversations will give you more energy to focus on the conversation in front of you.

- The Person Being Coached – Pay attention not just to the words but also to how the person constructs their thoughts, what emotions underlie what they're saying, their interests, attitudes, energy, motivators, etc. Get the full picture of the situation and trust your intuition if you sense that you don't see it or that more is going on than is obvious.

- The Environment – What's going on around you? Are there other things going on that are distracting you, either physically or mentally? If you're distracted, some strategies that might help you pay attention are to occasionally repeat back what the person has said to you, jot down what's distracting you, or create a visual in your head of what the person is saying.

Watch your airtime. Remember, of the 100 percent of words that are used, managers should only be accountable for about 30 percent of them while employees should account for about 70 percent.

Directing

You should use this strategy when a situation requires immediate action or you determine that this is the most effective way to move someone forward. But use this strategy sparingly, for two reasons. First, it's an easy one to choose and often the first one we pull from the tool kit without thinking whether it's appropriate. Second, the more we use it, the more we'll have to use it because we've created a conditioned response where people come to us first for answers. But sometimes the best way to get people to focus and move forward is to clunk them on the head with a big ol' set of directions. Use this strategy sparingly.

Giving Feedback
We'll discuss this in detail later in the chapter.

Practicing
Adults don't like to practice. But if I could make one shift in what people do to learn, it would be to get them to practice. Practice is a fundamental step in changing behavior, which is obvious in other aspects of our lives but which we're thick-headedly against in companies, and that drives me crazy. Here's the thing – practice works. Here are some practice tips for coaches to keep in mind:

- Provide scheduled times and a safe environment to practice.

- Where you can, use a project or content that's relatively low-level to practice on.

- Solicit feedback and provide feedback throughout the practice. (Volunteer somewhere and practice there!)

- Be the steward for patience because it's easy for both you and the person practicing to lose it.

- Make sure people practice.

Connecting with Resources
Sometimes you aren't the expert in an area that people need to improve. That's okay. You aren't expected to be an expert in everything. You are expected to help your employees find the right people or resources that can help them develop competence. You are expected to facilitate making connections and introductions for your employees or to ask others for ideas that might help them. Remember, the *Successful Manager's Handbook* is a great resource for ideas on how to

develop employees, as is *FYI (For Your Improvement): A Guide for Development and Coaching* by Michael Lombardo.

I was coaching the general manager of a Brazilian business. We were in a plant and strolled out into a field as we spoke about growth opportunities for that business. He told me he really wanted to branch out but didn't know what direction he was going to take the business. He said he thought there was an opportunity for a white sauce business in that market. I didn't know how to build a white sauce business but I knew someone who did. I pulled out my cell phone and called the president of a business located in France. I told him I was standing with the president of the Brazilian business and that he wanted to understand how to develop a white sauce business. Coincidently, the president of the French business had told me a few weeks before that he wanted to grow his white sauce business outside of France. These people had similar styles and work ethics and I knew they would get on famously. I ended the call with a commitment from each of them to have a conference call the next day to begin the discussion. Connecting people to resources is sometimes all that's needed from a coach.

Teaching

I can't do justice to the topic of teaching in a few paragraphs. I have a master's degree in teaching so I'm fully aware of the comprehensiveness of the discipline. But here are a few tips I'll offer because occasionally you may have to do some teaching.

Adults learn differently from children. Knowing these differences (adult learning theory, pioneered by Malcom Knowles), you can adjust your approach to get more bang for your buck. According to adult learning theory, adults are autonomous and self-directed, have life experiences and knowledge they bring into learning situations, are goal-oriented, are relevancy-oriented (must see a reason for learning), are practical, and need to be shown respect. When any of these are compromised or violated, the adult learner shuts down.

To learn, people need to have an interest in the subject matter. Tap into their motivation to learn as a leverage point. Reinforcement is essential and can be positive or negative. Employees have so many things vying for their attention and retention. To increase the likelihood of retention, use a combination of approaches including visuals, auditory elements, and kinesthetic elements (doing something with it). Using only one of these elements usually results in retention of only 10 percent of the information, whereas if you use all three, and maybe add in the responsibility to get them to teach it back, the retention goes up to 70–80 percent. Wow! That's a huge difference. Makes you want to be a little more intentional in how you structure the learning process! It's important that teaching is done well, and yet it's often done poorly.

Because knowing how adults learn is important to actually helping them grow, here are a few more principles to keep in mind:

- Adults decide for themselves what's important to be learned.

- Adults need to validate the information based on their beliefs.

- Adults expect what they are learning to be immediately useful.

- Adults have much experience to draw upon and as a result may have fixed viewpoints.

- Adults are a tremendous resource for the teacher and trainer.

Sharing/Storytelling

Telling stories is a great way to help people learn concepts. You've seen storytelling used many times in this book as a way to further or clarify a point. Stories are memorable and make concepts easier to grasp. Anyone can tell stories given some good guidelines and practice. There are a number of good books on the market that can help if you aren't great at telling stories.

If you want to be a good coach, then develop competence in using all of these strategies. I'm barely scratching the surface with these overviews. Having good skills in these areas will provide you with more tools to help people develop. There is such rich literature and so many ideas on the above topics that I recommend that you create a project plan, tackle one topic per month, and learn as much as you can about it.

Step #3

Help employees practice.

It's pure craziness to expect someone to know how to do something, and do it well, if they haven't done it before. If a tennis player has played their whole life using their forehand and suddenly you tell them to use their backhand, it won't be pretty. Even professional tennis players who have a good backhand work daily to make it better. So why do we find such a reluctance to practice in the workplace?

There are several reasons for this, the first being that we're dealing with adults. Adults have pressures and expectations placed on them. While children are perceived more as blank slates, adults have experiences and opinions that influence what they think and how they process information. Another reason is that there are always time pressures. Practice takes time. Additionally, most managers don't understand how to help their employees practice. The net result is that most employees don't practice.

I was in Naples coaching the head of a business a few years ago. He was making an important presentation the next day to the executive team. While the executive team knew of him, they hadn't had much exposure to him, so it was a real breakout opportunity for him. He knew the subject matter very well. To be fair, he was a good presenter, particularly compared to others who would be presenting the next day. This individual was important to me, and I knew he was capable of being amazing. He said he'd practiced in his room. He'd also done a walk-through of the presentation with his team a few times. When I asked him how he felt regarding the conversation, he said he felt good. He said he felt comfortable and ready. But I wasn't letting him off the hook. I told him to meet me in the presentation theater that evening after evening activities. He reluctantly agreed.

We met at 10:00 P.M., and he began his presentation. I let him go on for the first two minutes of the twenty-five-minute presentation and then stopped him. I was informed but uninspired by his presentation. When I worked one-on-one with this individual he was amazing. He was enthusiastic. He had a great accent. He had a wonderful face, kind eyes, and a smile that added warmth to each experience with him, but that was when we worked one-on-one, and that was all missing in those two minutes. So I made him start over. I talked to him about what was missing – that the special characteristics that made him unique and powerful weren't showing up. Where he put his hands, how he used his hands, the inflection in his voice, etc., were all tools he unconsciously used daily that endeared him to people, and he lost them when presenting. It wasn't bad. It just wasn't amazing. I was going for amazing.

So I had him start over. We got through about thirty seconds of the presentation this time before I stopped him. I told him what was better and then emphasized what was missing. He started again and got about fifteen seconds through, and I stopped him again emphasizing what was better and what was still missing. I had him do it again. I stopped him at fifteen seconds again. He had presented magnificently so I celebrated it! He was ready to plow on and I said, nope, do it again. I had him do that first fifteen seconds a dozen times until he fully understood what we were trying to achieve and had it down cold. Then we moved on to the other parts of the presentation. We were so clear on what he was working on that I didn't need to go through the entire presentation like that because much of what he learned at the beginning of the practice carried forward. We spent about three hours practicing his already pretty good presentation. He wasn't happy with me, especially when I made him come to my suite and do it again at 7:00 A.M. the next day before he did it for real.

As you've probably already guessed, he was amazing. He stood out from the crowd ten-fold, whereas before he would have been only one or two times better than everyone else. He caught the eye of the CEO, who later referenced what he had said a number of times and remarked on the passion he had in getting his ideas across. The executive team respected that he had a clear point of view and took a stand. He was precise, correct, compelling, and memorable. Because of the impression he made, people paid more attention to him going forward. In a succession discussion shortly after, he was considered a viable candidate for several roles for which he previously had not been a serious consideration. I know this because, before the presentation, I had suggested his name for those roles and my recommendation was met with a lukewarm reaction. When I suggested his name after the presentation for various roles, there was an enthusiastic response. He finally came around on practicing. He was reluctant to do it at first, but he saw the difference it made.

During practice, positive reinforcement is essential. A basic tenet of behavior change is that if a behavior is rewarded, it's likely to be repeated. Verbal reinforcement serves as an accepted and common reward while people are practicing (that's why I celebrated the successful practice in the example above). Create a positive scenario for practice that includes sending positive messages when they get it right. Your efforts will pay off faster if you do.

I'm not one to overdo preparation. I prefer moving fast and taking on big challenges. With that said, I still consider practice to be one of the key determinants of success.

The bottom line is that practice should not be considered optional. It's necessary. It's vital. Even when you have someone who's skilled at something, a laser focus on what they're doing and ways to improve is hugely beneficial.

Step #4

Let employees know how they did in addressing the issue.

One of the biggest challenges in changing is knowing how much to change. When we do something, our brain quickly calibrates what feels right, what feels comfortable. The challenge comes when something we feel is right needs to be more or less than what it was. Movement away from the original calibration feels wrong, and we feel compelled to go back to the old way because that's the way that feels familiar.

I was coaching my son one day when he was working with one of his top horses. His elbow was sticking out away from his body, not where it should be. I had told him about it a number of times. He made a slight adjustment, moving it about an inch into his side. The problem was that it needed to go in much further. When I continued to tell him about this, it became less about his elbow and more about me nagging him.

The issue was that he didn't understand how much of a change was needed. It's the trap employees fall into with managers. Managers will say, "You need to be a better team player." Employees will try ABC things but in reality the manager was looking for XYZ behavior. Specificity is important not only when outlining what needs to be changed but also in defining how much has or has not changed.

Circling back to the example with my son, it wasn't until I videotaped him from behind that he clearly understood how much change was needed. As an aside, my two children are serious equestrians on their way to being two of the top riders in the United States. They insist on having each competition videotaped. After their rides, they hop off and grab the camera to see what they did well, how the horse was jumping, and what they will need to do differently next time. These videos are sent that night to their trainer, who works with them outside of competition. He watches the videos and calls them early the next morning, before the competition begins that day, to discuss their performance. This has been one of the most influential elements of their success – the immediate feedback on how they did, viewing their performance, making adjustments, and going at it again.

If a video camera isn't appropriate to help you calibrate how much change is needed, there are many other ways. One calibration tool I often use is, "On a scale of 1 to 10 with 10 being the best you've ever seen and 1 being the worst, how was that …?" Another is to ask, "Is what you just did more effective or less effective than what you did previously?" Sometimes I compare the change to miles per hour to make it easier to understand: "Your effort was about three miles per hour when you need more like seven miles per hour." I often liken change, especially behavioral change, to the volume button on a car radio. Sometimes turning it up one small notch or down one small notch makes the music resonate more comfortably in your ear. Having a number of calibration tools in your pocket is useful because different things resonate with different people, particularly when you're working across cultures.

Marshall Goldsmith, a world-renowned leadership expert and coach, uses a technique called a mini survey. I've had the opportunity to work with Marshall on several occasions. I hired him as part of a leadership program I designed with Tuck Business School. I've used him as an executive coach. I'm certified in his coaching methodology. I've used many coaches from his network of coaches for people inside organizations who needed a dedicated coach. I've used several of his books as prework to various programs. One of my favorites is *What Got You Here Won't Get You There*. My point is that I've had exposure to him in a number of ways and his thought leadership makes him a great resource for people trying to advance. In essence, he encourages people who are working on changing a specific behavior to query their stakeholders via an e-mail once a month for six months. In the e-mail, they say something like "I've been working on improving XYZ. Over the last thirty days, have you seen me do more of that or less of that? What ideas do you have for continued improvement? Thanks for your support as I develop myself in this way." Just by reaching out and broadcasting what you're working on, and then soliciting input, you'll get a positive reaction. Then by having your stakeholders answer these questions repeatedly over time, you are actively changing their perception of you in relation to the area you're developing. It's genius, fast and simple.

The bottom line here is perspective. Being a coach is about providing insights and paths to take someone's competency to a new level. The most successful leaders have figured this out. Mark Flemming is a general manager at a large consumer packaged goods company. Two of his greatest attributes are his humility and his quest for improvement. "I personally benefitted from the use of an executive coach. I found that experience to be one of the two most beneficial developmental experiences of my life. What I got out of the experience was feedback on the soft skills that truly determine success in an organization. I received feedback I had never heard before and probably would never hear from a manager. My coach and I talked about topics I don't believe most corporate managers would ever discuss with an employee – the fine points of my interpersonal skills, what the clothes I wear say/portray about me, etc. Shortly after the engagement, I was promoted to vice president."

Make people accountable for being better. Some are afraid to be better, strangely enough. Some executives need an external force to help them be more accountable to themselves. Carl Malloch is president of Malloch Construction, Malloch Group, and Proline Realty, a successful construction enterprise. This successful construction executive wouldn't be where he was in building a successful operation without the help of a coach. "I have had a personal coach for a long time. I set goals every year and most likely wouldn't reach them without a coach to hold me accountable."

One of the greatest coaches I know is Paul Valliere. He's an equestrian coach who's trained winners of World Cups, Olympic gold medals, National Finals, and more. My children have trained with him since Michael was seven and Hannah was five. He is like no other. As soon as my children step into his arena, they raise their game automatically. He expects it. He expects them to work hard, apply what he's teaching them, and win. He is skillful at evaluating situations very quickly. He'll then communicate any issues he sees and they'll go to work on improving them. He'll teach them how to do something correctly and give ongoing feedback about whether they're on track or not. Sometimes his feedback gets a little yelly when he's passionate about something. He drills down to the smallest level of detail and behavior during practice. And he actually makes them practice. Repeatedly. When they do something correctly he'll say, "Great, do it again to make sure it wasn't luck." He's a tyrant and a marshmallow. He claps, he yells, he laughs, he hugs. He cares. If you're serious about improving your riding, go to him. But go only if you're serious. He's not going to waste his time, and it's not going to be all rainbows and puppies for you. It will be hard work. But in the end, you'll be better.

Paul isn't perfect. But he works to be authentic and the best he can be every day.

I aspire to this level of coaching. I pride myself on being an excellent coach based on how hard I work at it and the success I've had. But I'm successful because I care. I don't work with people who don't have good character and serious intent to become better. I love helping people find more within themselves. Coaching is about them, and unless they're ready to do the hard work required to develop themselves, I'm not interested. When they are, they get a force of nature as a partner. I had an executive (now CEO) refer to me as the Dragon Slayer because I would address all the taboo and difficult issues that stood in the way of this person being successful, many of which were inside this person. I coach as if I have one foot in the coaching world and one foot in a waitressing job. I take personal risks and think that, if I have to, I'll waitress to support my family. With five degrees from universities, I hope I won't have to, but I would if it meant doing the right things in helping someone and in being straightforward versus not.

What kind of coach do you want to be? What kind of impact do you want to have? Those are essential questions you need to ask yourself before you look at raising your coaching game. The other essential element of being a great coach, after you determine the impact you want to have, is to become a *feedback master*.

Providing Feedback

Providing feedback is where coaching all comes together, or it all falls apart. You can do all of the prior stuff, but unless you're coaching someone who's committed to helping another reach a higher level, unless you're coaching someone who's good at positioning ideas so people can hear them, unless you're coaching someone who's willing to listen, or better yet, actively seek input, coaching just doesn't work. And even worse, your coaching might create other issues. People don't like feedback, especially formal feedback. They become angry with the feedback provider or withdraw from the discussion. Most employees are *very* threatened by confronting their weak spots. Feedback is usually seen as negative, but positive feedback is at least as important. The sad thing is, providing feedback really isn't that hard. It just takes good technique, commitment, and practice. Let's blow away the ideas that feedback is yucky and coaching is difficult.

Earlier I referenced the results of Corporate Leadership Council research on coaching. They've also done quite a bit of research on feedback. They found that employees who receive fair and accurate feedback from their managers perform nearly 40 percent better than employees who do not.

First and foremost, successful feedback has nothing to do with you, the giver, and everything to do with the receiver. If you want to be excellent at giving feedback, you must adopt this as a guiding principle. The focus is to give input to people about the absence or presence of a behavior or result that's working or not working for them. You want people to know what worked, so they can repeat it, as well as what didn't work, so they can course correct.

What I find funny is that I can clearly spot the people who are surrounded by a force field that deflects attempts at feedback. These people are obvious, and we encounter them throughout our lives. Parents take note! Start early and give feedback often so future managers (and society!) don't need to deal with the bad behaviors of your little Johnny when he's all grown up. Many behaviors that stand in the way of people's effectiveness are ones they developed at an early age, and these may take some effort to change.

I was on a plane from Boston to Dallas, on my way to work for a client. As I went to get into my seat, I had to get past the guy in the aisle seat next to my window seat in first class. The man was on the phone, with earphones in, and he was speaking quite loudly. As the plane filled and prepared for departure, this man stayed on the phone. All of us in first class were participants of the meeting he was holding. We understood that there were past due invoices and that while "not looking to do a science experiment, they need to get a sense of how many of those past due invoices were related to some type of billing error …" Blah blah blah. All the while he was carrying on, his tone was condescending and pompous. Two groups of people were simultaneously impacted by this behavior. The first group, the people on the phone, had to muddle through his input, squash their reactions, and still get things done. The people on the plane were the second group affected. In the twenty-five minutes we sat there, everyone in the cabin made some type of gesture that indicated frustration with his behavior. As we prepared to depart, he hung up. He then engaged in other loud behaviors such as constantly snapping his newspaper or dramatically turning pages. As I put my headphones on to remove myself from his impact, I thought, what do the people at work do to remove themselves from his impact? Does he know? Who's helping him with these offensive behaviors? I concluded that probably no one was touching this guy with a ten-foot pole. And there lies the issue. (P.S. He ate his lunch and typed on his laptop the same way, making loud chewing sounds while dramatically pounding on the keys.)

People are often not aware of their impact. And most avoid difficult conversations about the subject. In the workplace there are many barriers to having straight conversations. Deadlines, lack of knowledge, lack of skill, competing priorities, ego, and intent are just a few. However, one of the biggest sources of contention and frustration people have when working with others is that they don't know where they stand. Or, if they know, they've been alerted to it in a way that causes them to be defensive and angry. Getting good at giving feedback is an essential skill. My most common coaching question is, "Have you spoken with this person about the issue?" Most of the time the answer is no. That seems like pure insanity to me. How can you expect people to change if they don't have a clue about it? Not only do people not talk about things in a timely manner, they let things fester and, as a result, secondary issues are often created. It's all so unnecessary. Having a conversation with someone about a situation, and doing it with the right intent in your heart and mind, is easy. Having a kid battle cancer … that's hard. It's all about perspective. And the good news is that giving feedback gets easier and better the more you do it. So, practice!

If you're the one providing feedback, you can be more successful if you play it out ahead of the actual conversation. Things don't sound the same coming out of our mouths as they do in our heads. Talking it through with a trusted advisor or sounding board is a good way to prepare. If that isn't an option, try writing it out to organize your thoughts. Here's a form I use to organize my thoughts when there's a feedback opportunity.

FEEDBACK FACILITATION FORM		
Key Questions		
What do I want the person to do, know, and feel at the end of this session?	Do:	
	Know:	
	Feel:	
What should I avoid?		
What are potential ways this can derail?		
What types of language or specific words should I use to help?		
On a scale of 1 to 10 (1 = not at all)		
How much do I anticipate a problem?		
How much do I expect the feedback to cause change?		
How willing am I to give feedback?		
Other thoughts?		

Knowing that it's necessary but incredibly difficult for all sorts of people, feedback should be given with care. I believe it's a gift. The receiver has a choice on whether to use the gift or put it in a drawer. There are certainly consequences for not using it, but the receiver has the choice. Your job as the giver of feedback is to choose a gift that's useful and relevant and wrap it in such a way that the receiver is compelled to open and use it.

How do you go about doing that? Several elements need to be in play.

Focus on behavior or results. People can't argue with those. They either under-delivered on a target or they didn't. They either spoke while another was speaking or they didn't. These results or behaviors are easily seen or heard. That's the territory you should stay in; avoid judgmental language or broad statements.

You've probably heard about focusing on behavior or results before. But I can't emphasize enough how important this is to a successful feedback conversation. People are primed and ready to be defensive, at least internally, when someone is giving them feedback. This is especially true for adults. When you start by making broad statements – you're a poor team player or you have a bad attitude or your communication is terrible – people will react negatively because the language is inflammatory. Train yourself to stay away from this kind of language when you're providing feedback. You don't need the headache of managing a strong reaction because of how the feedback was packaged.

Starting or stopping behaviors can seem overwhelming. One approach to giving feedback that's more palatable is to think in terms of "more of or less of." Don't tell someone that they must stop interrupting but rather that they should interrupt less often. This milder approach nets a better reaction from people as you broach the idea of changing behavior.

It's also important to provide context when you give feedback. Here you can add a little more subjectivity. For example, when addressing someone walking into a meeting ten minutes late, you could say it shows a lack of commitment. Or you could mention that it creates a perception that these meetings aren't important. Speaking about feelings or perception is acceptable in establishing context.

It's important to be specific in your feedback. Anyone can make general statements about anything, but that doesn't make them true.

My kids know that if they want to give me feedback on something, they better have it nailed down in terms of what happened and when I did it. Armed with that information, they'll get a dialogue in return and often an apology if I've unknowingly offended anyone. Without it, they don't have a chance. It works the same way for anyone who works for me. I demand quality and specificity. If you're going to tell me there's an issue, you need to be specific.

That leads us to another important element, which is suggesting ways to improve. If you have ideas, then help the person by sharing them. You don't have to be an expert.

Soliciting Feedback

I have a love/hate relationship with feedback because I want to be perfect in so many things. I know I need input so I'll know how I'm doing, but I really don't like being told what to do.

With that confession out of the way, I know that to achieve the most, I can't be a wimp. I must *actively and intentionally* solicit feedback so I know what I'm doing right and what I'm doing wrong. So I ask. I don't wait for feedback to be given to me. I don't wait until I've done something egregious, when I would have to deal not only with that but with an uncomfortable feedback situation as well. I go after it with a baseball bat. I want to know, before others know, so others don't know. It's crazy, but many executives are wired this way. It can come from being naturally curious or inherently defensive. As a manager, a key to helping you be successful at managing is proactively soliciting feedback.

The good thing about soliciting feedback is that the more you do it, the easier it becomes. After various meetings or events, I always ask, "Is there anything you would like to see more or less of next time? Anything I could have done to make this better that I didn't do?" Using these questions quickly conditions the people around you to think this way, and soon you'll be engaging in an ongoing dialogue with them. Dialogue is key. I'm smart enough to know that I need to get continual feedback to calibrate my internal assessment of the situation with the external reality. This thinking is typical of most successful people. If you're engaged in ongoing dialogue then you don't have the awkwardness of *the feedback session*. (There should be dark music played here.)

Being proactive is a good strategy in soliciting feedback. You can't be dependent upon others to provide it. You need to ensure your success by making sure you have clarity on how things are working and how you are being perceived. While it's a reasonable expectation that a manager fulfills their responsibilities in providing feedback as a manager, there are no guarantees that you have a good manager. The CEO of Hasbro, Al Verrecchia, put it well one time at a lunch he and I had with employees every month. One employee asked him how to handle having a manager who didn't help with development and wouldn't give the person feedback. He said, "Everyone has a turn in the pickle barrel at having a bad manager. The trick is to figure out how to be successful in spite of that. No one will look at your poor performance and under-developed skills and say, 'Well, that's excusable because you had a bad manager.' They will just think you're a bad performer or under-skilled and move on." Own your own performance. Make sure you get the coaching and feedback you need.

Using Intuition

One of the keys to my coaching success is intuition. I mentioned at the beginning of this chapter that good coaching was a head, heart, and guts proposition. Here's where the guts come in.

Most people are afraid to make mistakes. They find it hard to rely on hunches, feelings about things that just come to them. They don't listen to their intuition.

Don't get me wrong. The more objective and concrete you can be, the easier things are to understand and modify or repeat. Washing your hands is a behavior. Coming to the 7:00 meeting at 7:10 is a behavior. Asking five close-ended questions to shut someone down and diminish their contribution is a behavior. Thanking someone for his or her contribution in a meeting is a behavior. Recognizing these things makes it easier for you to repeat them or modify them.

But the best coaches also use their intuition in feedback situations. They have the courage to put out ideas that are kicking around in their heads, about why something is happening or what someone is thinking. That's intuition. Grabbing onto the sense of something, grabbing onto something that's running through your subconscious, pulling out the thing sitting in your stomach, that's using your intuition. I've had the biggest breakthroughs with people when I've relied on my intuition. Testing those hunches often leads to good dialogue.

Intuition-based questions or statements such as these have worked for me:

- I have the sense that there's more to this than you're telling me. Is there more?

- I'm sensing that there's an issue we haven't addressed. Is there?

- You've mentioned XYZ briefly in the past. Could that be playing a bigger role than maybe you realize?

- What are you afraid of?

- What's the voice in your head telling you right now?

Be attuned to the obvious and not-so-obvious undercurrents around you. Intuition involves being aware on a number of different levels.

If you're going to rely on intuition you have to be okay with making mistakes. It's common to second-guess yourself because of past experiences. Try using your intuition on a smaller scale to build your confidence. Listen to non-verbal messages and your internal voice when it speaks to you. If you keep at it, your ability will develop over time.

FeedForward

A fundamental challenge with feedback is that it focuses on the past and the past can't change. There's a school of thought that says that to focus in this way is static and limiting. The premise of feedback is that, by understanding the effect of our past behavior and actions, we can adjust them to get more favorable results in the future. There's also another way.

FeedForward is a concept designed by Marshall Goldsmith, whom I mentioned earlier. I'm a fan of Marshall because he has simple ideas that are easy to implement and they work. His common sense approaches to leading and managing are easily grasped in his books and lectures. He freely shares his information because he is very much committed to broadly helping people improve.

Marshall is a proponent of focusing fully on the future rather than reflecting on a past that you can't change. The goal is to get suggestions on how to be successful in a given area in the future. You get a group of people (although it can be done one-on-one) who are focused on development. They each identify one development area that they're working on and solicit ideas on how to improve. They each need to meet with as many people as possible in the group in the time allotted (based on the size of the group) and do these things:

- Say hello and do a quick name/function introduction if necessary.

- Say, "I am working on XYZ. What suggestions do you have for me to try in the future to improve this area?"

- Respond with "Thank you."

The receiver of the information cannot debate it, explain anything in relation to it, or look like they're assessing it. They can only say thank you. The exception is if they don't understand the suggestion. Then they can ask for clarification. The person offering suggestions doesn't need to be an expert and shouldn't feel pressured to offer perfect recommendations. It's sometimes from the strangest starts that the best things happen.

A common reaction to this exercise is that people are amazed by how much they can learn from people they don't know. People also genuinely enjoy this exercise. Often, in other approaches, constructive feedback promotes defensiveness and negativity, whereas this approach is almost always seen as positive because it's solution-focused and not problem-focused.

Marshall says that there are eleven reasons to try FeedForward:

1. We can change the future. We can't change the past.

2. It can be more productive to help people be right than prove that they were wrong.

3. FeedForward is especially suited to successful people. Successful people like getting ideas that are aimed at helping them achieve their goals. They tend to resist negative judgments.

4. FeedForward can come from anyone who knows about the task. It doesn't require personal experience with the individual.

5. People do not take FeedForward as personally as feedback.

6. Feedback can reinforce personal stereotyping and negative, self-fulfilling prophesies.

7. Face it – most of us hate getting negative feedback, and we don't like to give it.

8. FeedForward can cover almost all of the same material as feedback.

9. FeedForward tends to be much faster and more efficient than feedback.

10. FeedForward can be a useful tool to apply with managers, peers, and team members.

11. People tend to listen more attentively to FeedForward than feedback.

I found that a combination of FeedForward and feedback works best. People find value in understanding context, but they don't want to be beaten over the head about it. So when giving feedback, offer only enough examples to help them understand. State the issue in terms of behavior or performance and the result. Create a dialogue rather than a soliloquy.

Managers need to be transformational and therefore must have strong feedback skills. I was coaching an executive in a program at Harvard, and he casually mentioned as part of a larger conversation that his manager was not a fan of performance management and feedback. My internal voice replied immediately, "Then he needs to be fired." To me it's a black and white issue based on my experience around the world. Rachel Neo, a development consultant, talks about a program called Game-Changing Leadership. "We designed and rolled out this program to 1,000 leaders within the UK&I business, inspiring people to take personal accountability for making small changes every day, including providing feedback. It created a culture of performance and a commitment to personal development." Small changes over time lead to big results. Start today.

The Chapter's Big Ideas

- Coaching is helping someone reach a higher level in the areas of performance, career, development, and behavior.

- Feedback is giving input on something that happened.

- Coaching is who you are, not something you do. It's a mindset and a skill set.

- Feedback is a gift. It should be delivered with positive intentions. People have a choice on whether they will use it or not.

- Coaching consists of four steps:

  1. Help employees understand their current situation regarding an issue and why it's important to address it.

  2. Help employees understand how to change their situation.

  3. Help employees practice.

  4. Let employees know how they did.

- Fill your tool kit with many coaching strategies so you'll have the right tool to help someone advance. Strategies include asking, listening, directing, giving feedback, practicing, connecting with resources, teaching, and sharing/storytelling.

- Practice is essential.

- FeedForward is a terrific technique to provide input and insight without some of the potential negatives of feedback.

- Take time to plan your feedback. Organize your thoughts using the Feedback Facilitation Form or something equivalent to help you have a productive session.

- Intuition plays a major role for many good coaches.

COACHING AND FEEDBACK ASSESSMENT

On a scale of 1 to 10, with 1 being not at all and 10 being at an industry standard level, rate your organization on the following questions:

	LOW								HIGH	
	1	2	3	4	5	6	7	8	9	10
1. How often does quality coaching occur in your organization?	☐	☐	☐	☐	☐	☐	☐	☐	☐	☐
2. How committed are people to helping others grow?	☐	☐	☐	☐	☐	☐	☐	☐	☐	☐
3. How well received is the idea of feedback in your organization?	☐	☐	☐	☐	☐	☐	☐	☐	☐	☐
4. How competent would your team say you are at coaching?	☐	☐	☐	☐	☐	☐	☐	☐	☐	☐
5. How competent would your team say you are at feedback?	☐	☐	☐	☐	☐	☐	☐	☐	☐	☐
6. How often do you use a range of tools/coaching strategies when coaching someone?	☐	☐	☐	☐	☐	☐	☐	☐	☐	☐
7. How much do you rely on your intuition in coaching situations?	☐	☐	☐	☐	☐	☐	☐	☐	☐	☐
8. How much do you insist on practice with the people you are coaching?	☐	☐	☐	☐	☐	☐	☐	☐	☐	☐
9. How often do you stop and intentionally plan the feedback you're going to provide?	☐	☐	☐	☐	☐	☐	☐	☐	☐	☐
10. How often do you give positive feedback compared to negative feedback?	☐	☐	☐	☐	☐	☐	☐	☐	☐	☐

COACHING AND FEEDBACK ACTION STEPS

For anything you rated less than 9, what are you going to do about it?

Question #	Actions to Take	Timeframe	People to Involve

PART IV

Additional Components

CHAPTER TWELVE

Motivation and Style

ONE OF THE MOST IMPORTANT leverage points you have as a manager and leader is a person's motivation. When you tap into a person's drive to succeed, you open a world of possibilities.

This idea of motivating or inspiring others can come across as somewhat mystical. It's not. Let's break it down. When we find people inspirational, we identify something in them that draws us to them. It could be achievement, an attitude, or a communication style. This something incites us to reflect and perhaps be more than we were. Since people are different, it stands to reason that there are many types of people who can motivate or inspire us. When that motivation taps into our passion, it can be very powerful. Passion carries its own fuel.

My last manager at Heinz, Steve Clark, the Chief People Officer, clearly understood that. He knew that I loved my work and that it was my life's purpose to help people develop. He also understood that money was a huge motivator for me because it funded my kids' Olympic dreams. I over-delivered on my already aggressive responsibilities so I would receive an increased bonus. He would tap into my drive to help the organization achieve success. The company benefited by the significant amount of discretionary effort I chose to contribute. Steve set me

PERCENTAGE OF EMPLOYEES WHO ARE HIGHLY DISENGAGED

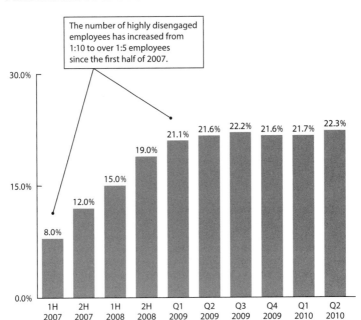

The number of highly disengaged employees has increased from 1:10 to over 1:5 employees since the first half of 2007.

Exhibit 12-1. Source: IMF World Economic Outlook, October 2009; Reuters, "Consumer Confidence Slips," 26 July 2010; Bureau of Labor Statistics, "Organization for Economic Cooperation and Development," 26 July 2010.

up with clarity of purpose and the room and incentive to over-deliver, and everyone benefited.

Managers face a difficult time trying to motivate or inspire employees in today's work environment. Exhibit 12-1 shows how more and more employees are becoming disengaged, and disengaged employees are almost impossible to motivate or inspire.

This graph shows us that more than one in five employees are checked out. Because of their higher level of disengagement, people are giving their companies less extra effort. Discretionary effort is the amount employees choose to give above and beyond what's required to get the job done. With high levels of engagement, employees are motivated to give more discretionary effort, resulting in higher levels

200

of productivity for the organization as a whole. It pays to keep your employees engaged and motivated.

Research on motivation resulted in the Herzberg Two Factor Theory. It's the most widely known and used framework when it comes to motivation. The theory says that employees' motivation ranges from being demotivated and dissatisfied, to being neither satisfied nor motivated, to being motivated and satisfied. Employees have certain expectations of employers, and those basic expectations are referred to as hygiene factors. They include company policies, quality of management, pay rate, job security, relationship with others, and the overall work environment. Many people expect that pay will be high on an employee's list of motivational factors, and for some it is. But for most, there are other factors that are valued much higher.

In a study that McKinsey & Company did on motivational factors in the workplace, pay was the most frequently used motivational tool but the second least effective out of six tools. Ranking above pay were achieving results, having the opportunity to advance your career and personally grow, receiving recognition, having a keen interest in the work you're doing, and being given appropriate responsibility and room to do the work. Providing these will result in a highly motivated, more-engaged workforce that will help the business be successful.

Managers are smart to create an environment that's built on tapping into people's motivation. People who are motivated actually motivate others. The sad reality is that managers consciously or unconsciously do things that result in employees disengaging and becoming demotivated. Teach people how to win. Success breeds success. Richard Chang's *Passion Plan* is a good book to help you figure out how to do this for yourself, and his *Passion Plan at Work* can help you bring passion fulfillment to your workplace. These books will help you sort through this pursuit in a logical, well-thought-out way.

One of my past teams and I developed a significant program for leaders in a large global organization. The intent of the program was multifaceted. One objective was to get a bench of leaders established for the next generation of heads of functions in various countries or to raise the skill set of existing leaders in those roles. Another was to establish a baseline of expected skills across this organizational level. Yet another objective was to get together leaders who were in similar roles across the company around the world to network and establish relationships. This program was a big step for that company. As I kicked off the program, right in front of me was a leader from Venezuela. He sat as close as he could to the front of the room, with a pad on his lap and a pen in his hand, looking straight into my eyes. He stayed that way through the yearlong program. He was the first in and the last to leave. He thanked us profusely every time we met, and he brought chocolates from Venezuela each time a new phase of the program started.

I had many occasions to work with him as a result. Once when we were chatting, I told him that it was wonderful to run such a program and have a participant who was so engaged. He explained to me that what we were doing was important to his team in Venezuela. He shared that it was critical to find new ways of working and new ways of leading people because the socio-economic environment was so challenging. He wanted to learn everything he could so he could bring it back to his team members who didn't have this opportunity that he had. He was always grateful and always smiling. This had a positive effect on my team. We always wanted to help him. We always wanted to do more to equip him to raise his game and the game of his leaders. The person assigned to be his coach for the program freely spent time with him, coaching him on various issues as they came up. He ended up turning around the commercial organization by applying what he learned. We promoted him to be managing director of the Venezuela business, and he tried even harder.

People like this are contagious. You want to be better as a result of working with them. You also want to do what you can to help them. His boss and I discussed plans for me to work with his leaders in Latin America. His boss wanted me to spend time in Venezuela since it was one of the most important businesses in his region. I had no desire to go, truthfully, because the reported kidnapping and murder rates made me nervous. It wasn't until I worked with this individual that I felt compelled to go. I put my faith in those two to keep us safe and made the trip. (I arrived the morning that president Hugo Chávez secretly returned from Cuba for the last time before his death was announced, so it was an interesting time to be there.) My visit was incredibly appreciated because almost no one ever came to this business. I know I wouldn't have gone if I hadn't seen all of this individual's hard work and the great momentum from his efforts. He inspired me to the point of putting my misgivings aside. That's the power motivation has.

Positivity Goes a Long Way

Don't underestimate the power of a positive environment. High-performing managers with high-performing teams will tell you that keeping an optimistic, forward-looking approach will work much better for you than creating a hostile, fearful environment. Life is too short to not enjoy it. People work hard and spend a great deal of time at work. Being positive is a choice. It's easy to get pulled into the downside of things. Resist the temptation.

Fostering a positive environment doesn't have to be complicated. For example, at Bank of America a survey on employee engagement showed that recognition needed improvement. The bank instituted a practice that, for the first five minutes of every meeting, the group needed to recognize people. In the summer at Hasbro employees could work longer days Monday through Thursday so they could leave at 11:00 A.M. on Friday. Also at Hasbro, the company would rent a movie theater and show previews of movies that we had the license to make toys for in order to create excitement and followership. The company got back in effort much more than the small cost of renting the movie theater. Little efforts over time result in big benefits and lots of loyalty.

Sometimes Less is More – Getting Out of People's Way Can Be a Huge Motivator

As managers, we're conditioned to *do*. But sometimes manager involvement is a demotivator.

Before speaking to your direct reports ask yourself, "Will my involvement make this person more, or less, committed to doing a great job?" If the answer is "less committed," then ask yourself, "Does the value added by my contribution exceed the loss in commitment from this person?" If the answer is "no," don't get involved.

Before speaking in team meetings, ask yourself, "Is this comment going to make our team more effective, or is it just intended to prove that I'm more clever than my peers?"

If the primary driver of the comment is your own ego, don't speak! Sometimes you should just get out of people's way.

Tap Into People's Motivation

Isn't it obvious that we would want to know what's important to an individual – money, vacations, prizes, or intangibles such as pride, honor, and love – so we can leverage that motivation? Sometimes when I ask managers what motivates their employees, they'll name general things. When I ask if they know what motivates a specific individual, say Dylan, they often can't tell me. When I suggest that they ask the employees, many managers get uncomfortable. Let's see how a manager's conversation with Dylan might work:

> Dylan, I'm working on being a better manager so I can help everyone on my team reach their potential and enjoy huge success. To that end, I want to create a positive environment where people feel motivated and inspired. I know different things motivate different people. What motivates you? When do you find yourself most inspired? When do you feel the most excitement about accomplishing things?

In my experience, if you have similar discussions with your team, they'll engage quickly. If you haven't had conversations of this nature, your team members will probably be a little surprised at first. However, when managers engage like this, it sends a good message. Very quickly employees see that and respond well to the discussion. My advice to managers is to give it a try. What's the worst that can happen? The employee is suspicious? Then have your actions follow your words. The employee is slow to engage? Then ask more open-ended questions to draw them into the conversation.

If this is pretty far from how you typically operate, send an e-mail first. The e-mail might look like this:

> Dear Dylan,
>
> I've been thinking a great deal about how to get our team to the next level, and one area I'd like to get some clarity on is what motivates each person on the team. I want to create a positive environment where people know what's expected of them, feel motivated to achieve, and are able to contribute to their highest level. Because people are motivated and inspired by different things, I would appreciate you reflecting on the questions below. Let's discuss them this week.
>
> - What motivates you?
>
> - When do you find yourself most inspired?
>
> - What demotivates you? When do you lose energy, get frustrated, and find your passion drained?
>
> - What role do you want me to play? How can I help you get the most out of yourself?

A top performer I worked with previously, Raffaello Distefano, is now an executive at Loomis Sayles. He knows the role that motivation plays in helping people be successful and understands the value of knowing what motivates each employee. "In managing individuals, personalities can be challenging. Utilizing personality identifiers and understanding what helps drive such individuals to achieve was crucial in assessing and managing people. During review periods, spending a bit more time in listening and providing feedback is central to a person's personality profile. This paid dividends in having them achieve higher satisfaction in their positions. Some people required more handholding and continuous feedback whereas others wanted to drive a project on their own with a more hands-off approach from management. Getting to know your team is critical to having a more satisfied workforce."

Steve Clark, a manager I previously mentioned, tapped into my motivation not only by feeding my incentive needs but also by playing to my style. Steve and I would agree on desired outcomes and then he would step aside. He was always there if I needed anything or wanted a sounding board, but he didn't create unnecessary work for me. He trusted my decision-making and was essentially egoless, so he gave me and my team the room to be successful. He got great outputs as a result. Steve clearly understood that, although I'm great at working with my team, my partners, and my clients, I hate to be managed, so he created an environment that allowed me to thrive. Understanding people's style, combined with tapping into what motivates them, is pure genius.

Managers often don't understand what motivates people. I've seen managers use fear (oh, the stories I could tell you!). Sometimes they're hands-on for a given situation, but then disappear. And sometimes they treat all their employees the same as though everyone were motivated by the same factors. These are all common mistakes managers make – avoid them.

In my role as head of diversity in a few organizations, I've been responsible for the annual Take Your Daughter to Work Day. The first time I had this responsibility I decided to let the folks who had been running it do it as they had in the past because the event was coming up soon. The event was boring and got low marks from the kids. It was essentially a babysitting effort for forty kids who were out of school during April vacation and came to work with their parents. What a missed opportunity.

About six months before the event the following year, I launched a survey to the parents of children who might attend. The survey asked whether they attended in the past, why or why not, what they liked, what would they like, what advice did they have, etc. Armed with data, I pulled together the planning committee who had worked on the event the last five years. The feedback was not well received by the planning committee. New suggestions and advice were discarded on the grounds that they wouldn't work, that it was good enough last year, etc. I interrupted the meeting and acknowledged the efforts of past years and thanked them for carrying the torch for this event. I then said that the data spoke for itself and things were going to change. It was clear that we had a huge opportunity to positively impact girls during a very influential time in their lives. I told the group that I was going to solicit new volunteers from the company who wanted to create something transformational, and whoever in the existing group wanted to be part of that, I would love to have them.

A new committee was formed. There was one individual who was passionate about the event and had many useful ideas. I asked her to be the lead. I got some pushback from other people in the organization because she was an administrative assistant. I didn't care. She had the skill and will to get the job done. I shared with her my vision. I solicited her thinking on where we should take things. I gave her the standards by which I thought we would be successful and told her that we had to hit those marks. I also told her she was in charge. We set up weekly meetings so she could use me as a sounding board.

The event was an over-the-top success. Two hundred children attended, which was five times the number from the previous year. We had fun events, workshops on different functional areas so the kids could think about different careers, guest speakers who spoke briefly, food donations from Nabisco, pictures to remember the event by, lunch with parents, etc. It was amazing. We surveyed the kids and then the parents of the kids after the event and received a 4.8 on a 5-point scale as well as suggestions for the next year's event. What made this event successful? We tapped into people's motivation. They wanted to be part of something significant and we gave them room to make a contribution. That's an excellent formula for success.

We've seen how to motivate others directly. We can also motivate indirectly. I wanted Bill Johnson, CEO of Heinz at the time, to attend an event in order to send a message to company leaders who were going to be there. He was incredibly busy. I told him I would make him a deal. If he came, I would make homemade chocolate chip cookies for him (a major weakness of his). He agreed. The morning of the meeting Bill's assistant said he probably couldn't make it. I handed over the package of homemade cookies and asked her to give it to him along with a sealed note. The note read, "I upheld my part of our bargain." A few minutes after we kicked off the session, guess who joined? It made all the difference in the world to the participants. Given today's challenges to get people's time or attention, sometimes a small gesture can make all the difference in the world. Homemade cookies aren't what got Bill to the meeting. Homemade cookies sending the message that this meeting was important served as his motivation to attend the meeting.

What Makes Someone Inspirational?

Inspiration is a great motivator. If you say, "I'm not the type of person to inspire others," then you're probably underselling yourself. Inspiration comes in many forms, from many people, from many places. As I spend time speaking with people on this topic, I find I'm pretty typical in this regard. I find inspiration in many ways from many sources. The examples below show you some of the traits and behaviors of people who have inspired me and motivated me to work hard. (The traits and behaviors are in italics.)

- **Jim Shanley,** former head of leadership development for Bank of America, is incredibly inspirational. He's got a *down-to-earth-style* and loves the time he spends on his farm. He's also a well-respected thought leader because he has a *clear point of view,* and his *firm conviction* makes him compelling. Jim called me after reading an article in *HR Magazine* about a program I'd created at Hasbro. I made the decision, after ten years, to leave Hasbro. I loved the company but, having been there for ten years, I needed a new, big hairy challenge.

  Jim called me on a Tuesday and said he wanted me to spend time with him and his team to see if I'd be interested in working with him. I was honored to have him call, since I already knew of him and respected him greatly. The trouble was, I had received five job offers from top companies that week. No joke. I had the good fortune to engage in a number of searches simultaneously and they all came together in that same timeframe. By Friday I needed to decide which job to take. I was leaving for London on business that night, landing Wednesday and flying home Thursday night. He told me to take the return flight to Charlotte, North Carolina, where he would make his team available to me on Friday. I did just that. At the end of the day, Jim pulled me in and said, "Listen. I want you on this team. I want you in this organization. I think you can be terrific here, and it would be great for you. His *directness, careful planning,* and *clarity* in letting me know what he wanted were overwhelming. I agreed to join in that moment.

- **Sandra Drought** was a serious force to be reckoned with at Bank of Boston. I had the incredible luck to join the Teleservicing business that she was in the early stages of transforming. She blew into a room with papers flying behind her, always dressed to the nines. She was *eloquent* and *intentional.* She banged on the drum about how important *attitude* was. She *thanked people* at all levels. In short, she was inspiring. Two weeks into my corporate career I caught the fever after meeting her, and I decided that I would do anything to be a part of what she was creating. And I did.

- **Jan Kruise,** a former colleague, is inspirational for many reasons. He was so convinced of the power of *tapping into and developing people* that he consistently defended his team and procured resources to make them successful. Jan took over the German business and *changed* the leadership team, installed SAP in nine months, completely *reinvented* the customer base, changed much of the talent in the organization, *dealt with* several significant legal issues that came from earlier decisions and actions, and *created* an organization that was incredibly poised for success. Jan created a "birthday" for the "new" company and asked me to be in Germany for the launch. I made sure I was there because Jan would get to leverage my visit for his people, because I wanted to feed his needs, and because he inspired me.

- **Al Verrecchia,** former CEO of Hasbro, was quite inspirational. He was a tough guy. He held his emotions close. He was a *straight shooter.* No nonsense. A finance guy at heart. You would question whether someone with such a style could be inspirational. He was for sure. His *clarity of intent,* his *transparency,* his *integrity* all created followership. He had a *strong work ethic* and a *compelling story* – putting himself through the state university while recently married and with a child. He started at the lowest level in the organization and worked hard. People would ask him what he did to position himself to be CEO. He said he didn't position himself. He believes he just had a little more *courage* than the next guy to take advantage of opportunities that were offered to him. He never got far from his roots. He and I would have monthly lunches with employees so he could *keep in touch with what was happening* in the organization. He would *respond to every idea and suggestion* that came during these lunches, and he'd *tell heartfelt stories* of his life, like the time that his little Italian mother chased him around the kitchen with a frying pan because he got too full of himself. He was easy to relate to, which made him inspirational.

  I asked Al to come to Dartmouth College where I hosted a leadership program at Tuck Business School. I asked him to teach the ethics class. His real-life stories helped the leaders *understand the trade-offs* a CEO has to make. He talked about a product that was the hottest-selling item at Christmas. All the stores were out. It was hugely profitable with significant back orders. And he had just found out that the factory that was producing them used child workers. Hasbro had a comprehensive approach to certifying factories, but somehow this one had gotten through the cracks. What would you do? If you moved production, the families of these child workers would have difficulty affording food because their work was a major source of income. If you stopped production, you wouldn't have time to move it to another factory with all the necessary machinery. He shared how challenging this decision was, but in the end focused on the fact that Hasbro makes the world smile and it's all about kids' welfare. The decision was clear – he needed to *do what's right* and shut production down. The program attendees were galvanized by these real situations and his *authenticity*. He created great followership along the way.

- **My parents** have a legacy of being inspirational, but in an unassuming way. They both went to Brown University. My father went after World War II (he lied about his age to get into the Navy to fight). My mother had to take four buses to and from the university. My father started work in a large, global, jewelry company as a box boy in the mailroom and worked his way up to run the company. My mother had ten children after she ran the Pediatric Teaching Department at Rhode Island Hospital. All of the children were at the top of their class, top of their sport. They all went to college (half to graduate school) and got married. When my parents had nine children under the age of fifteen in the house, they took in pregnant, unwed mothers to give them a safe place to live until the babies were delivered. When my father retired, he joined International Executive Services and went into third world countries to help turn around companies. My mother would travel with him and they lived as natives in these countries. Examples of their *hard work* and *caring for others* are limitless.

- **Roel van Neerbos,** with his Roel's Rules, created great followership. His *clear leadership principles* made him someone people wanted to work with and follow. He worked to *create something significant* as the head of Global Ketchup that inspired people.

- **Jeff Carney,** an executive at Bank of America, created tremendous energy with his *singularity of purpose* in working to establish a retirement business in the bank.

- **Vijay Gorvingarjan** and **Syd Finklestein** inspire students and leaders with their *unassuming ways,* their *simple yet profound messages,* and their *agreeable natures.* They're two professionals who have taught for years at Tuck Business School and other schools and businesses. They've written great books. For example, *Why Smart Executives Fail* is a must-read for all executives.

- **Jacques Pradels** tries to be a *good role model* as a way to create followership and motivate his employees. "'Whatever you are, be a good one,' said Abraham Lincoln. I think it is all about *learning and teaching,* with your own philosophy and *set of values. Coaching* is a great tool to help great leaders be better and successful, and I do my best to help them in that way."

- **McLain Ward** is an *expert* equestrian whose videos inspire my son, Michael. Michael watches them over and over again to keep in mind what a soft but *effective* rider McLain is. Because of his size (he's six foot four) Michael faces riding challenges in keeping his body quiet and in being successful at jumping big jumps. McLain rode with Michael's trainer for much of his life and won many national competitions, and now global competitions, including gold medals in the Olympics. So Michael endlessly watches McLain *to learn.* Hannah, Michael's younger sister who wants to be as good or better … watches Michael to learn.

Look at all of the different types of people who have motivated me and all the different ways they touched me. You want to be inspirational? Figure out where your passion and the world intersect and do that really well. *Act with integrity, reach out to understand* what's important to people, and then *lend a hand* to help them be better. That's inspirational. Carl Malloch, president of Malloch Construction, will tell you that it's simple: "Set a good example, set the bar high, and treat people right." Being motivational isn't some mystical skill. It's not complicated. It's showing up every day with a big commitment to excellence to something and touching people in simple or significant ways.

Engagement Surveys

One of the reasons that people leave companies, often one of the top three reasons, is that they don't understand how they contribute. They don't feel engaged or inspired or part of something. Creating a culture of engagement is a necessary element to having a motivated workforce.

Gregory Wagner of ValuEngager says it well: "Employee engagement is easy to do but often misunderstood. When not understood, many things are done in the name of employee engagement that are ineffective in creating higher productivity and lower turnover. It's not about happy employees. It's about creating an environment where each employee understands what the greater team is trying to accomplish. Understands their contribution to that end. Feels as though he/she is valued by the team and its leadership, and sees the team's goal as being something positive that makes them feel like they are part of something important that is bigger than just them. Everything a leader does to understand and create that environment will pay off huge. The key is understanding what employee engagement truly is …"

A formal or informal engagement survey can be a great source of input about what's working and what needs adjusting. Don't do a survey unless you're serious about responding to the results because, if you don't respond, your efforts will work against you. Inputs from surveys can help you create a high-performance environment. I use a framework that involves the concepts of skill and will:

Good Motivational and Managerial Practices
+
Meaningful Work
+
Setting Clear Performance Expectations
+
Use of Effective Rewards and Recognition
=
CULTURE OF EXCELLING

Style – Different People Require Different Approaches

Part of tapping into people's motivation is understanding their style. Being able to structure work and communicate in a way that resonates with people because you've packaged it in their style can be powerful. Dave Mitchell, author of the *Power of Understanding People,* tells you to "hire talent and lead style." Dave has designed a methodology coupled with an effective instrument that helps people understand themselves and their motivators as well as those of others. "Start with yourself. The best leaders also have the best metacognitive skills. Exceptional leaders understand themselves, know how to learn, and value the differences they experience when dealing with others."

I've used this instrument with several groups with great success and strongly recommend reading the book. The instrument is contained in his book and is free to use. It's simple to understand and powerful when applied. I've also used other instruments such as the Myers Briggs Type Indicator (MBTI), the Social Styles Indicator, and the DiSC Style Instrument. Each is unique, and some are more comprehensive (and complicated) than others. All provide insight into behaviors and preferences, which can help you maximize the value of your interactions.

Some leaders clearly see value in understanding style. Mark Hammond, a sales executive, has had lots of success by "expecting the best of each individual. Coach them on how to be their best. Be a constant student of their approach and style. Adjust your style to meet theirs. Listen listen listen vs. talk talk talk, and stay close to their style."

It's the give and take based on understanding styles that make for harmonious and highly productive teams.

Understanding style and context is often critical to the success of a task. I was in Dubai working with the president of a business there. I was delivering a custom report that integrated a 360 with a Hogan Executive Assessment. As a woman delivering feedback to a senior-level man in Dubai, I knew I needed to package the message so he could hear it and not be distracted by his cultural norms. Additionally, I had him complete an MBTI assessment to give me insight as to the type of language that would resonate with him and what his natural personality tendencies were. Doing the hard work to figure out how to get the message across paid off with a very successful meeting.

The bottom line is that you need to do what it takes to get the best out of people. Tapping into their styles and motivations is just smart business.

The Chapter's Big Ideas

- Passion carries its own fuel. Tapping into people's passion is just good business.

- Studies show that there's an increasing level of disengagement throughout the workforce and a decreasing amount of discretionary effort that people are willing to contribute to their organizations.

- People do things that inspire you to do things you might not otherwise do. It's contagious.

- Positivity goes a long way.

- Getting out of people's way can be a big motivator.

- If you don't know what motivates the people around you, ask.

- Inspirational people come in all shapes, sizes, and styles.

- Shaping things in someone's style increases their motivation to perform well.

- Little efforts add up to big benefits, such as loyalty, so grab the opportunities as they come along.

MOTIVATION AND STYLE ASSESSMENT

On a scale of 1 to 10, with 1 being not at all and 10 being at an industry standard level, rate your organization on the following questions:	LOW 1 2 3 4 5 6 7 8 9 HIGH 10
1. How well do you understand the various ways people can be motivated?	☐ ☐ ☐ ☐ ☐ ☐ ☐ ☐ ☐ ☐
2. How often do you tailor your motivational efforts to the unique needs and interests of the various people on your team?	☐ ☐ ☐ ☐ ☐ ☐ ☐ ☐ ☐ ☐
3. How well do you understand patterns of behavior that form a person's style?	☐ ☐ ☐ ☐ ☐ ☐ ☐ ☐ ☐ ☐
4. How often do you flex your style and package things in another way to match other people's style?	☐ ☐ ☐ ☐ ☐ ☐ ☐ ☐ ☐ ☐
5. How inspirational would your team say you are?	☐ ☐ ☐ ☐ ☐ ☐ ☐ ☐ ☐ ☐
6. How intentional are you about making yourself inspirational and engage in work with a mindset of motivating others?	☐ ☐ ☐ ☐ ☐ ☐ ☐ ☐ ☐ ☐

MOTIVATION AND STYLE ACTION STEPS

For anything you rated less than 9, what are you going to do about it?

Question #	Actions to Take	Timeframe	People to Involve

CHAPTER THIRTEEN

Diversity

WHILE THIS IS NOT A BOOK about diversity, you *cannot* have a conversation about talent management and development without at least briefly addressing diversity. To understand diversity you need to understand that people have different characteristics they can and cannot change. These characteristics shape the way people receive and interpret information and therefore behave. The variety of characteristics included in the diversity arena is vast. Diversity can be about differences in physical characteristics such as age, race, hair color, gender, etc. It can be about differences in background characteristics such as birth order, geographical upbringing, and accent. It can be about differences in business characteristics such as function, organizational level, and seniority. It can be about differences in characteristics as broad as ideology or as specific as sexual orientation. Regardless of the differences, the reality is that people have different characteristics, people are diverse, and that diversity needs to be managed.

At Hasbro, the tag line I created for diversity (Diversity at Hasbro) was D@H = people + products + profitability. It's a simple concept. When we get the people piece right, employees work together more effectively, especially diverse groups, and the outputs (i.e., products) are better. When the products are superior, very often profitability follows.

Research has shown that superior results come from heterogeneous groups vs. homogeneous groups. It makes sense, don't you think? When there are a lot of different ideas to choose from, the end choice should be better. The challenge is that with difference comes complexity. With difference sometimes comes conflict. Most people either don't like conflict or don't manage conflict well, so they shy away from diversity.

The reality is that if you do the things we've talked about in this book, you'll be more effective at managing diversity:

- If you care and are committed to helping people grow, you'll be more effective at managing diversity.

- If you set good performance expectations and take away ambiguity, you'll be more effective at managing diversity.

- If you check in with people to monitor their progress and make sure they're going to be successful, you'll be more effective at managing diversity.

- If you have the right incentives in place that are fair and equitable, you'll be more effective at managing diversity.

- If you're committed to being a good coach, you'll be more effective at managing diversity.

- If you have good feedback techniques, you'll be more effective at managing diversity.

- If you work to inspire and motivate others, you'll be more effective at managing diversity.

- If you work to flex your style to better connect with other styles, you'll be more effective at managing diversity.

When I was head of diversity at Hasbro, we won the Innovative Practice Award from the Society for Human Resource Management for a program we created. I worked with Dani Monroe, who is the person who turned me onto diversity work when we were at Bank of

Boston together. So when I was looking to build a program, she was an obvious choice as a partner.

We created a module that I call the learning-in-spite-of-yourself module. People don't like coming to diversity programs. They perceive them as high risk and forced. They often come in with an attitude – "What are you going to try to teach me about diversity?"

This program happened without employees even knowing that they were in a diversity workshop. Music played as they walked into the room, and they were immediately put into a group. Once everyone was there we played *Who Wants to Be a Diverse Millionaire?* This was based on a game that Hasbro was currently producing and a popular game show at the time. The questions asked were all related to changing demographics or diversity within Hasbro or the industry in general. It raised people's awareness on many levels. It was played in a light, fun, competitive manner that made the learning palatable.

From there we moved into an exercise using Pokémon cards. Pokémon was also one of our brands. People had to choose nine descriptors of themselves or create some on blank cards. The top three descriptors went in the top row. Ones for me would be female, executive, mother, and I would have written in "youngest of ten kids," "competitive horseback rider," "five degrees," "relentless," etc. Once the employees selected their nine descriptors and placed them in the plastic sleeve (if you've ever seen trading cards, it's the same sleeve), they got into groups of three for discussion. What happened next was amazing. People learned new things about others they'd worked with for twenty years. The exercise brought out aspects of people that were previously unknown. One person was no longer "the guy from marketing" but perhaps a champion swimmer or the dad of a special-needs kid or was running a foster home for dogs or had two elderly parents he was caring for, or wrote poems as a second job. There was so much more to each person in the room the others had never known. People wear their work faces to work so what shows up at work is generally a small piece of who the person is. Can you imagine if we harnessed the power of all that difference? Can you imagine if we brought our full selves and all that perspective to our roles in companies?

An interesting pattern emerged from that Pokémon exercise. Every woman took a woman card. Every person of color took a person-of-color card. Almost every woman and person of color had those cards in their choice of top three cards. Very rarely did men take the male card, and almost no one took a Caucasian card. When we asked why, the same answers emerged class after class. The men said that they didn't think to take the male card, and Caucasians said that they didn't think to take the Caucasian card. There were more interesting cards to select. However, women and people of color said it was obvious that they needed to choose those cards. They are reminded every day in every way that they are women or people of color. One African American woman said, "I'm reminded every time I look in a mirror that I'm a black woman and reminded in several interactions I have with people every day."

The room was always silent after this point in the conversation. Diversity isn't about judging, it's about realizing. It's not about converting, it's about what is. It's about creating room. Does everyone have the same opportunity to pull their chair fully up to the table to contribute and to reach their potential? When people don't feel comfortable, they hide and protect elements of their life. Think about the energy that goes out the window when someone is worried about what others will think when they leave at a certain time to pick up their children at day care (even though the person started work several hours before the others), or when someone avoids conversations about the weekend because it would reveal that they're gay.

Dani Monroe, the partner in designing the Hasbro program that I mentioned previously, has written a great book called *Untapped Talent*. It talks about the hidden workforce and their experience and the reality of poor talent management strategies that result in a population that is just "there." It's a great book exposing the powerful realities that could aid you in leveraging your employees even more.

Many of the challenges of managing a diverse group come from ignorance. People don't know all that's important to know about others, and they're afraid to ask. But we can only know by asking. I think of it this way: Imagine a coffee filter. You put coffee grounds in a filter, add water, and a good cup of coffee comes out. If you laced that filter with raspberry, the output would still be coffee, but it would be different. If you laced it with chocolate, the output would again still be coffee, but again it would be a bit different. The flavors in our filter are things such as marital status, parental status, education, ideologies, geography, birth order, organizational function, etc. As a leader, you must always remember that the only person having your experience is you. And you need to understand that there are lots of other types of experiences. Don't be afraid to bring people of difference in to help you understand different elements of your business. For example, it would be obvious to have a Hispanic person in the product development or marketing end of things when developing a line of business for the Hispanic market. You would be surprised how often this isn't the case. It sometimes requires perspective that can only be achieved through experience to provide insight into some dynamics.

One example of this occurred when I was working with the Mexican business at Hasbro. The Playskool vacuum was a big seller around the world. Senior management insisted that the Mexican business put more vacuums in their forecasts and increase their sales plan. They didn't and were seen as difficult and "doing their own thing." Immediately, stereotypes that exist for dealing with affiliates kicked in. When the Mexican business was approached about why they wouldn't take more of this product, they said it wouldn't sell. Their point was that many Mexicans will spend their lives as low-paid housekeepers. Parents didn't want their children to aspire to being housekeepers by engaging in play with vacuum cleaners because they wanted more for their children. Wow. Assumptions were made and frustrations were exhibited all around something that made perfect sense. The Mexican business wanted to be successful and have high sales as much as any other business. They just weren't going to be able to do it with that product.

I've worked with several senior leaders who have held their leadership teams accountable for being leaders in diversity. At Bank of America each leader had a diversity component in their individual development plans. At Hasbro each leader was monitored in their use of the paid time off that was given to them for volunteering every month, in order to encourage them to actually use the time. At Bank of Boston leaders were asked to sponsor different pieces of the diversity strategy.

New perspectives that come from managing diversity can be quite positive for the business. For example, the CEO at one big financial institution did a great deal of work on diversity when someone close to him disclosed that she was a lesbian. This changed how he looked at the workplace. One leader at Bank of America spent time doing work with the Hispanic market, which in turn gave him ideas on how to grow the business. One leader at Hasbro worked to get his team to use their volunteer hours to help build a playground for children who were differently-abled. This was an eye-opening experience for many. Many times, as was the case with the CEO at Heinz, senior leaders will look at things such as benefit packages to see how competitive they are in terms of diversity, especially when their daughters enter the workforce and complain that their companies are not responsive to them. Don't run away from diversity or ignore it. Understand that people have different experiences, make different choices, and follow different paths in life. Allow for different ways to get the work done. The more enlightened managers will take diversity further and seek to understand and use differences – the superior results those managers achieve are well documented.

The Chapter's Big Ideas

- Research has shown that superior results come from heterogeneous groups vs. homogeneous groups.

- The reality is that if you do the things we've talked about in this book, you'll be more effective at managing diversity.

- People wear their work faces to work. What shows up at work is generally a small piece of who the person is.

- Diversity isn't about judging, it's about realizing. It's not about converting, it's about what is. It's about creating room.

- Many of the challenges of managing a diverse group come from ignorance. People don't know all that's important to know about others, and they're afraid to ask. But we can know only by asking.

CONCLUSION

I WROTE THIS BOOK because I've been incredibly frustrated by people's experience in working for other people. When people are treated poorly at work and don't feel good about themselves, they go home to their families and children and friends spreading their unhappiness. When people lack clarity, direction, and feedback, they are unfulfilled. When people aren't linked tightly to driving the business, success is difficult to achieve. I want to see that change. I'm passionate about helping people become better today than they were yesterday. It's an honor and an inspiration. It's also good business sense.

Life's too short not to be great at the things you're doing. If you're a manager, treat the role with the sanctity that it deserves. Commit to ongoing learning and continuous improvement, for yourself and your employees. Good talent management practices work and make a significant difference in the lives of your employees and the success of your business. Be disciplined enough to put good practices in place and to consistently execute them. Create dialogue. Be real. Be authentic. Be a servant-leader. Fill the halls with laughter while hard work is happening. Keep it simple. Insist on positivity. Become an amazing coach. Unleash your potential while you're unleashing that of others. You and your employees deserve it.

INDEX

ABOUT THE AUTHOR

Kim Janson is the CEO of Janson Associates, a firm dedicated to helping teams, individuals, leaders, executives, and organizations be incredibly successful (www.jansonassociates.com). Kim also serves as a facilitator and executive coach for the Harvard Business School.

Prior to establishing Janson Associates, Kim was the Chief Talent Management Officer at the H. J Heinz Company. At Heinz she was responsible for leadership development, organizational effectiveness, learning, diversity, change management, performance management, succession planning, and executive coaching. She also has extensive talent management experience as a senior vice president at Bank of America, and as a senior leader at Hasbro, BancBoston Mortgage Corporation, and Bank of Boston.

While at Hasbro Kim won the Society for Human Resource Management's Innovative Practice Award for her diversity work, and she was featured in *HR Magazine* on the leadership development program she built in partnership with Tuck Business School.

In addition to being CEO of Janson Associates, Kim and her husband Mike run a very successful champion-level horse farm, Zanger Hill Stables (www.zangerhillstables.com).

Kim is a member of numerous associations including the Association for Talent Development (formerly the American Society for Training and Development), the Society for Human Resource Management, the United States Equestrian Federation, and the ASPCA.

COMING SOON

Becoming Top Talent

by

Kimberly Janson

Published by Maven House Press